AN OREGON SCHOOLMA'AM

BOOK TWO

— The Depression Years —

CALAPOOIA PUBLICATIONS

LINN COUNTY, OREGON, COMMUNITY HISTORIES
By Margaret Standish Carey and Patricia Hoy Hainline

BROWNSVILLE: Linn County's Oldest Town
HALSEY: Linn County's Centennial City
SHEDD: Linn County's Early Dairy Center
SWEET HOME IN THE OREGON CASCADES

OREGON NONFICTION
By Grace Brandt Martin

AN OREGON SCHOOLMA'AM
From Rimrocks to Tidelands
AN OREGON SCHOOLMA'AM: BOOK II
The Depression Years

COVER PHOTOS

Author's 1928 school application picture
Paulina schoolhouse with cattleguard in foreground

AN OREGON SCHOOLMA'AM

BOOK TWO

— *The Depression Years* —

by Grace Brandt Martin

Calapooia Publications
Brownsville, Oregon

Dedicated to my supportive friends,
particularly Simon Johnson,
whose expert advice was always available to me
during the writing of this book

AN OREGON SCHOOLMA'AM: BOOK II
THE DEPRESSION YEARS

Calapooia Publications, publisher and distributor
27006 Gap Road
Brownsville, Oregon 97327

ISBN 0-934784-26-4
Printed in the United States of America

Second Printing, October, 1982

TABLE OF CONTENTS

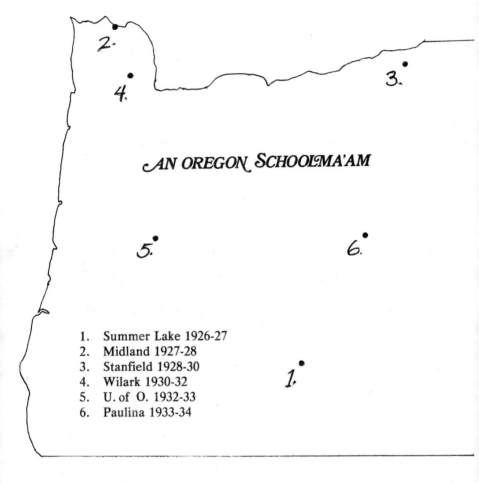

AN OREGON SCHOOLMA'AM

1. Summer Lake 1926-27
2. Midland 1927-28
3. Stanfield 1928-30
4. Wilark 1930-32
5. U. of O. 1932-33
6. Paulina 1933-34

Partial map of Oregon, showing approximate locations of the various schools referred to in Grace Brandt Martin's two "Oregon Schoolma'am books."

FOREWORD

An Oregon Schoolma'am, Book Two: The Depression Years is the second of two books written by Grace Brandt Martin about her experiences as a young Oregon school teacher, beginning with the years just before the nation's Great Depression and continuing through the depression years.

The author's first two years after graduating from normal school took her from the one room Summer Lake school in the high desert country of southeastern Oregon to Midland, a two teacher school served by a school boat along the Columbia River tidelands. She tells of her experiences at Summer Lake and Midland in her first book, *An Oregon Schoolma'am: From Rimrocks to Tidelands.*

An Oregon Schoolma'am, Book Two: The Depression Years continues Grace's story from 1928 with two years at Stanfield, near Pendleton; two years at a logging camp called Wilark, in the Oregon Coast Range; a year at the University of Oregon in Eugene; and a year at Paulina, in the ranch country southeast of Prineville.

Grace Martin has quoted from journals kept during her teaching days to help recreate the mood of the times she writes about. The reader will again follow the development of this fascinating young woman as her attitude and outlook become even more sophisticated, while she continues her struggles to maintain her high standards at the tail end of the Roaring Twenties and into the Great Depression.

STANFIELD
1928-1929

As I packed my trunk late in August of 1928, I was preparing to leave for my next teaching assignment. I already had earned two years' experience as a teacher in two contrasting areas of Oregon. After graduating from Oregon Normal School in 1926 I taught my first school—a four pupil, one-room school—at Summer Lake, a remote, semi-arid cattle ranching community in south central Oregon.

The following year I was principal of the two-room school, as well as upper grade teacher, at Midland, an island in the Columbia River, approximately forty miles upstream from where the river flows into the Pacific Ocean. Since Midland is not far from Clatskanie on the mainland, its school was under the jurisdiction of Clatskanie's school system.

Now I would soon be on my way to Stanfield near Pendleton in northeastern Oregon, a completely different part of the state. From what I had been told about the town when I was hired by its new superintendent, I thought I would probably feel more at home in that location than I had in the two previous places where I had taught. There were a few cattle and sheep ranches in the district, but most of the people lived on a reclamation project where intensive farming, including truck farming, was carried on. Having grown up on a small acreage in the suburbs of Portland, where my father in his spare time grew a large kitchen garden each year, I was certain that I would be more knowledgeable about truck gardening than I had ever been about stock raising in Summer Lake or fishing or dairying on Midland Island. And after my parents bought and moved to a farm near Gresham, I became all too familiar with the problems, financial and otherwise, faced by the full-time farmer.

I was looking forward to the coming year for several reasons: first and foremost, because of the excellent annual salary of $1,200 for a nine months' school term in contrast to prevailing Willamette Valley teaching salaries of $800 (or less) to $1,000. Then too, I would be teaching one grade in a town school which was a definite step upward professionally. And not to be forgotten was the thought that in Stanfield I might have opportunities for an interesting social life as well as a change from the coastal lowlands' excessive rainfall.

The last day in August I boarded the train which left Portland at 11:00 p.m. and was due to arrive in Stanfield at 6:00 a.m. The next morning while I was in the Pullman dressing room making myself ready for whatever the day might bring forth, two young women joined me. I soon learned that they were teachers returning to Stanfield for a second school year and when I told them that I, too, would be teaching in Stanfield, they looked me over with curious interest.

"Do you know where you'll be staying?" they asked.

"I have no idea," I replied, "but I'm expecting Mr. Kelty, the new superintendent of schools, to help me find a place."

Their reaction to this was to tell me smugly that they were staying at the best boarding place in town. Then one of the young ladies—the one with a small, close-fitting hat stylishly covered with feathers—hastily added, "Of course there isn't room for anyone else at our boarding place."

By now the train had pulled into Stanfield—or to put it more accurately—had come to a stop at the depot on the outskirts of the little town. We all got off. Immediately my fellow teachers became involved in enthusiastically greeting a young man waiting there with his car, but they *did* stop long enough to answer my questions as to the whereabouts of the hotel. After that, all three climbed into the automobile and soon were out of sight.

I looked around me in the early morning silence and saw that there were no paved streets or even sidewalks in this part of town. Later I was to learn that there were no paved streets anyplace in town, unless one called the paved surface of U.S. Highway 30, which passed through the business district, a paved street. The shade trees around each house had been planted there, for this was a desert country where sagebrush was the principal natural vegetation. However, across the tracks I could see broad irrigated fields of alfalfa and green pastures dotted with white-faced cattle.

Even this early in the morning the sun's rays were warm. The birds were singing in the locust trees, and I was conscious of the smell of sagebrush and the fragrance from the adjacent alfalfa fields. I noticed smoke floating into the sky from the chimneys of a few early risers. The air was clear, the sky was a deep blue, and I was glad that I would be teaching in eastern Oregon again.

Mr. Kelty had written to tell me that I should wait for him at the hotel so I picked up my suitcase and walked over there to await his coming. It was a small, unpretentious establishment with a screened porch covered with hop vines and beyond that an open front door leading into the lobby. The proprietor heard me come in and assured me that I was welcome to stay there until the school superintendent showed up. One and a half hours later I was still there. I had looked through all the reading materials in the rack (most of which were dairy and livestock magazines) and was feeling bored, hungry and neglected.

Then a smiling Mr. Kelty arrived and greeted me warmly. During the ensuing conversation I realized that my companion, who was also a newcomer to Stanfield, had no definite boarding place for me in mind. By the time we reached his car, I was feeling extremely anxious for I had never forgotten how I went from door to door looking for a place to stay at Summer Lake where I taught my first school. I fervently hoped that I would not have to go through a repetition of that worrisome experience here in Stanfield.

However, when I mentioned my encounter with the two young teachers, that seemed to help Mr. Kelty decide upon a course of action. He started the engine and drove over to the graveled street that the young man at the railroad station had taken earlier. He headed in the same direction, so I suspected that he might be going to the same place. I hesitantly informed him that I'd been told there was no more room where the young ladies boarded, but this didn't faze Mr. Kelty. He resolutely continued on his way. We passed through the center of town which consisted of one main street (U.S. Highway 30) and a few short side streets lined with tree-shaded houses, then continued on approximately a quarter of a mile outside of town, past fenced-in, sagebrush-covered fields in which I noticed outcroppings of alkali.

A large, square, one-storied house, painted white, came into view even before we left town because it was built on a knoll surrounded by open fields on three sides, making it stand out from the rest of the landscape. As we drew nearer, I saw that it was located upon a plot of ground approximately one-half acre in size enclosed with locust trees planted along the entire perimeter. The dwelling sat in the center of a small, well-kept lawn in the far corner of the grounds. The rest of the place was unirrigated and covered with tall weeds. This place proved to be Mr. Kelty's destination.

After he had driven up the long driveway, we got out of the car and followed a cement sidewalk across the lawn to the house. There we were met at the kitchen door by a pleasant, black-haired middle-aged woman. Mr. Kelty addressed her as Mrs. Sloan, and after introducing me inquired if she would be interested in having another boarder. This called for some careful consideration so she led us out of the roomy, sun-flooded kitchen through a wide central hall leading to the living room and asked us to sit down. Then she went away and came back with three young ladies whom she introduced as Sue Shepherd and Margaret Templer (both of whom I had met on the train) and Gertrude Lawrence, who had been a classmate of mine at Oregon Normal School.

The three knew why Mr. Kelty and I were there and eyed me warily as an interloper come to spoil their harmonious set-up. Mrs. Sloan showed her gift for diplomacy by assuring them that it would be up to them to decide whether or not there would be a fourth boarder. After that I had the unusual experience of listening to them as they argued against taking me into the household.

First, Gertrude protested that she would have to share her room and the one full-sized bed with me. But this point didn't carry much weight because Sue and Margaret had only one full-sized bed in their room. All of them continued to rack their brains in an attempt to think of every possible reason why an additional person in the household would be undesirable. This is one I have never forgotten:

"But, Mrs. Nettie," (that apparently was what they called their landlady) "if we have another boarder, you'll have to cut the pie into smaller pieces."

Mrs. Sloan calmed their fears. "That wouldn't be much of a problem if I made a little extra pie for me to eat. Then I'd cut the big pie into five pieces, as I did last year, and you'd have exactly the same amount."

The rest of their arguments were just as expertly countered by Mrs. Sloan so her boarders finally gave up. The matter was settled. I would not have to look further for a place to live that winter.

Since our trunks had not arrived, there was little to do that first forenoon, so Sue and Margaret decided to take some books over to the high school, and they invited me to go along. It pleased me to be included because the seventh grade classes were held in the high school building, and naturally I wanted to see where I would be teaching.

The high school was located on a low-lying patch of ground which was separated by a pasture from the last house on that street, which was really a graveled county road. Large plots of fenced-off land lay across the road and on two sides of the schoolgrounds. On our way there we had followed an unimproved lane about a quarter mile long which led from the county road in front of Sloans to another county road in front of the school.

Stanfield High School building, 1928

As we walked through the brick school building, I realized that it was an exceptionally fine one for such a little town. It boasted an auditorium for entertainments with rows of seats sloping down to the stage complete with splendid blue velvet curtains and gray backdrops. Next to the auditorium was the gymnasium large enough for basketball games. On the second floor I saw an inviting little library, stocked with what was then considered a good supply

of books. There was also a small science laboratory, the superintendent's office, and a teachers' lounge which doubled as the school's
health room. And in addition to classrooms for six teachers on the
two floors, there were some unused ones for an eventual increase in
enrollment.

The seventh and eighth grade rooms were grandly called the
"junior high school," although, in reality, all there was to it were
two rooms on the ground floor in one end of the high school. I
learned that Wayne McGowan, a 1926 graduate from the Oregon
Normal School, would be the eighth grade teacher. Like all of the
teachers—excepting Mr. Kelty and me—he was returning to Stanfield after having taught there before.

As the girls showed me around, they informed me that most of
the grade school pupils and high school students came by bus from
farms on the irrigation project and outlying sheep and cattle ranches. On our way home they pointed out the gray stone school
building on the other side of town where Mildred Bush, Leora
Devin and Gertrude taught the first six grades.

During the first afternoon of my stay in Stanfield, my roommate, Gertrude, took me around town, but there weren't many
places to visit in order to be presented to people.

There was Refvems' General Merchandise Store, Shooks' Drug
Store, the post office (in the same building with the pool hall), a
small family-style restaurant, Billups' Garage, and if you were
there on the right day in the week, a barber shop. The liveliest place
in town was the pool hall, but of course we didn't stop in there, nor
at Mr. Billup's Garage, for that matter. I also saw a few empty
business buildings, including a bank, so assumed that at one time
the community had been more flourishing.

We dropped in at the home of the town's telephone operator who
lived on one of the side streets. As Mrs. Greathouse entertained us
in her living room where the switchboard was, our conversation
was frequently interrupted as she put through calls. A pleasant
person, she was visited as much for her personality as for her
knowledge of what was going on in town and around the
countryside.

We did not have many business places to visit, it's true, but my
introduction to the community took most of that Saturday afternoon because farm people were in town to do their weekend shopping. We encountered them in the stores and on the street, and
Gertrude, who had taught there the two previous years, stopped to
visit with anyone she had ever known.

With everyone to whom I was introduced, it was always the same: they were eager to know of my past experience as a basketball coach. They were especially interested because the girls' basketball team had won the county high school championship the year before and, according to all the enthusiastic supporters I talked with, they could do it again if they were well coached. Between encounters Gertrude explained to me that the high school boys' prospects for having a winning team were poor, so the school patrons were depending upon the girls to uphold the town's honor.

I knew perfectly well why I was being quizzed about my history as a coach. When I decided to go to Stanfield I had unconcernedly signed a contract for a teaching position that included, among other duties, the training of the Stanfield High School girls' basketball team.

The awful truth was that I had no previous experience as a coach, and my ability as a basketball player had been unimpressive during gym classes in elementary and high school. And later, when I tried out for a position on an intramural team at Oregon Normal School, I was guarded so closely by a stalwart, fiercely competitive girl that my height—my one definite asset in the game—gave me no advantage. Playing opposite that determined adversary left me intimidated and permanently stripped of any illusions about being an accomplished player. Now with this background I was expected to lead the Stanfield girls to another county championship.

It had all seemed so far in the distant future, and coaching sounded like a relatively unimportant responsibility when Mr. Kelty and I were discussing the matter back in Columbia County during the preceding spring. But on that September afternoon five months later, I knew how badly mistaken we both had been. My heart sank as I realized that I could not escape the day when my inability as a coach would become apparent not only to the girls on the team but to their loyal fans. So it was a relief when Gertrude ran out of people to talk to and took me back to our boarding place.

During the following week I was able to push the inevitable showdown to the back of my mind and feel enthusiastic about the present.

September 9, 1928

Here I am at Stanfield, the place where I had such a time deciding to come to. This school system is considered one of the best in Umatilla

County. Of all these little towns along the Umatilla River—Echo, Hermiston, Umatilla, and Stanfield—this town has the most modern school buildings. At least the high school building, where I'm holding forth, is. Being an up-to-date two story brick structure, it seems like heaven to my Summer Lake and Midland-accustomed eyes.

My boarding place is very comfortable and well-furnished. It has a furnace, bathroom, and electric lights so I'm not so far from modern conveniences as Mama predicted I would be if I came to Stanfield. Mrs. Sloan is a dear and an ideal landlady because she doesn't "bother" herself about having boarders. She's been "keeping" the town's teachers for several years and understands people our age. The board is thirty dollars a month.

The other girls here at the house are Gertrude Lawrence, whom I knew slightly at Normal School and is about my age, Sue Shepherd, who is 23 and a graduate of the University of Oregon, and Margaret Templer, 24, also a University of Oregon graduate. Gertrude teaches the fifth and sixth grades. The other girls teach in the high school which has four teachers including Mr. Kelty. They are all lovely girls and fun to be around, but I feel more "soul matish" with Sue.

My diary's thumbnail sketches of the people in the household were far from complete. For instance, I did not mention our landlord, Mr. Frank Sloan. Mr. Sloan was an unusually big but well-proportioned man whose exact height I have forgotten, but I do recall that when I stood by him, I felt almost petite.

Born in Morrow County fifty-nine years before that time, he had been engaged in sheep or cattle ranching all of his adult life. That fall he was raising sheep which he pastured in the Blue Mountains during the summer and wintered on his sheep ranch several miles from Stanfield. He was a respected and prominent citizen of the area and at one time had been its representative in the Oregon State Legislature.

Our conversation around the dinner table generally dealt with school or community happenings, but occasionally Mr. Sloan added depth to the discussion by guiding it around to world politics and business conditions. As a result of listening to his well-informed comments, we gained an insight into the events of the day which we probably would not have had if left to find it for ourselves.

The Sloans had two grown children: Rachel, who was teaching at Pilot Rock, near Pendleton; and Bill, a senior at Oregon State College.

Mrs. Sloan, Grace Brandt's landlady at Stanfield

I soon discovered that Mrs. Sloan had a good sense of humor and treated her boarders impartially. If she had a favorite she never allowed the feeling to become apparent. We were also certain that she and her husband were loyal and would not gossip about us, any more than they would talk about the members of their own family. I soon joined the others in their conviction that this was "the best boarding place in town."

2

On the opening day of school the temperature was 106° but I did not mind because I was buoyed up at the prospect of teaching one grade with an enrollment of only seventeen pupils, over half of whom were bright, well-behaved little girls. I loved the class from the start and the feeling seemed to be mutual although the boys were less demonstrative in their acceptance of me.

I wrote appreciatively of my seventh graders every time I took pen in hand to write in my diary during the first weeks of school.

September 9, 1928

My seventh grade is really truly a jewel.

September 16, 1928

The seventh grade continues to be angelic. It is an usually good grade.

October 17, 1928

My seventh graders are spending all their energy filling Junior Red Cross boxes for the poor urchins over in Guam. That seventh grade is *darling*. Some of them had lovely report cards to take home. A couple of the little girls (Florestine and Jureta) said they had never had better ones.

Early in the year this ideal situation, in which I enthusiastically taught a small group of cooperative pupils came to an end when Mr. Kelty asked me to take over the eighth grade classes in grammar and spelling. The eighth grade teacher would then teach arithmetic to my seventh graders.

Wayne had thirty pupils in his room with only a few girls, one of whom was definitely a trouble maker, and several of the eighth graders were reluctant learners as far as grammar was concerned.

I have two classes in the eighth grade room and, oh me, but what a task those classes are! So far it's been a struggle to get myself heard above the din because the little dears don't know that I'm supposed to be the captain of their ship. However, I can't let them bluff me so something drastic will have to occur before long.

The eighth graders are looney with adolescent love affairs and just plain insolent.

Another week has gone by and I'm still surviving. However, I must admit that I'm losing weight because dumb-like I'm letting those eighth graders get me down. It's my job to overcome their devilish tendencies but even the drastic methods of corporal punishment do not do the trick. I've tried it. What haven't I tried! Persuasion, bullying, coyness, everything. So far all have failed to win them over to my side.

On September twenty-eighth I was hopeful that they were coming around and beginning to like me, but by the middle of October I wanted to throw in the sponge and ask to be relieved of this unpleasant assignment.

Now I know that I was working at a disadvantage from the start because Wayne and I were entirely different types of teachers. Wayne, ahead of the times, was more relaxed and permissive than I, so when I went into his room and tried to conduct a quiet, structured class, his pupils didn't take kindly to my efforts. In fact, many calmly ignored the grammar assignments which were to be worked on during their study periods after I left, and there didn't seem to be much I could do about it—except to hand out poor grades.

Finally, I asked Mr. Kelty to let us return to being responsible for only our own pupils.

November 1, 1928

No longer does Miss Brandt struggle with the eighth graders. Perhaps I showed the wrong spirit in giving up but it was *so* much worry to me. Everything goes along smoothly now if I only can get out of coaching basketball. Really what I know about coaching is nil, for I have *never* been in a real game, only practice games, and few coaching points did I glean from them.

As the basketball season approached, I borrowed a book on

coaching from the friendly young high school science teacher, Ike Woodhouse, who also served as boys' basketball coach. I intently studied diagrams of plays and pictures of different foot movements, including methods of pivoting, used to evade a pursuer without being fouled. This pivot was my favorite and only accomplishment, which I practiced in Mrs. Sloan's roomy kitchen before dinner time while my housemates sat watching me, making humorous comments all the while about reading a book to learn coaching.

When the day of reckoning arrived, I met in the gym with the girls who made up the team, and with as much authority as I could muster, declared that the first activity would be to practice pivoting. The girls nonchalantly executed faultless pivots for a while and then looked expectantly to see what next I had in mind. Then I asked them to line up and throw baskets because logically that would be something that even a championship team might need to do. I followed that with other exercises I remembered seeing in the coaching book.

Finally the practice session came to a close. I walked home despondent from the knowledge that my performance had lacked authority. I was merely going through the motions without actually understanding what I was supposed to be accomplishing with the girls, and they knew it. I wish that I could report that, with time, I improved and led the girls to victory, but such was not the case. My charges were not disrespectful, but after a few sessions I sensed their growing impatience with my fumbling efforts, and I was not surprised when Mr. Kelty told me that they wanted Wayne to be their coach.

I'm sure that Mr. Kelty was pleased to find a solution to the awkward problem because now the basketball team, their fans, and Mr. Hoskins, the chairman of the school board, were happy again. As a board member, Mr. Hoskins used his considerable influence to encourage the development of winning teams, and besides that, he was the father of the star on the girls' team.

As far as I was concerned, I was immensely relieved but still not lighthearted, even though I no longer had to worry about teaching the eighth graders or coaching the high school girls. Now I was troubled by the thought that twice I had been tried and found wanting and therefore was a disappointment to Mr. Kelty and the school board, and worse yet, that I might not be rehired.

3

It didn't take long for me to perceive that I had been sadly mistaken in assuming that adventures awaited me in Stanfield. At Midland I had been dissatisfied with the opportunities for entertainment, but compared to the social life that I saw around me in Stanfield, Clatskanie (where I had spent most of my weekends the year before) had been the center of a veritable whirl of gay activities.

> September 9, 1928
> So far I haven't seen any "eligibles" around town. However, one can't expect too much of life—a good boarding place and *everything.*

> September 16, 1928
> This town is going to make me into an old maid yet, I fear, for there just aren't any young men around except the very few who already are going with one of the other teachers. Oh well, this way there won't be any cause for people to gossip about me.

> December 10
> The other girls have all gone, or are going out with their gallants. Naturally Sue and Gertrude are out with Vernon and Carl, and tonight Margaret has a date with Mr. Billups who owns the local garage.
> That exhausts Stanfield's list of eligible men, so I shall keep my customary role as the shy, sweet young thing who remains at home.

Most weekends Gertrude and Sue were on the go with their beaux. Gertrude was keeping company with a widower in his late thirties who owned a farm out on the irrigation project. His two pre-adolescent daughters were being brought up by Carl's two married sisters, who also lived out on the project, so Gertrude frequently went along when Carl visited them. In Stanfield there weren't many places to go or things to do except to visit people or go for rides over the desert, so this is what Sue and her beau, Vernon Waid, did, except that they added interest to the car rides by hunting jackrabbits.

Soon after I became Mrs. Sloan's boarder I learned that the handsome young man who had met the train that first morning was Vernon Waid, Sue's boy friend. He was in his middle twenties and lived in town with his parents when he was not working on a ranch.

Sue Shepherd, standing beside Vernon Waid's "Whippet"

One afternoon I found out what the more popular girls did to pass the time on weekends.

Today Sue prevailed upon me to be a third party so I accompanied her and her boyfriend on a long ride. We rode for miles over sagebrush country and shot jackrabbits. Vernon is the type that shoots jackrabbits when he goes jackrabbit hunting, so although Sue and I would rather have ridden on and on, he'd stop every once in a while to take a shot. Sometimes he let us shoot too, but we weren't as successful as he was.

Margaret's life was not a great deal more interesting than mine. Occasionally Mr. Billups, the garage owner, called her to ask for a date, but then again he didn't. While Sue and Gertrude were away most of the time weekends, Margaret and I stayed at home feeling left out, but we seldom joined forces to find something interesting to do because we didn't have the same interests, or maybe we were just plain incompatible.

After I had laundered my clothes, shampooed and set my hair with waterwave combs Saturday morning, I had taken care of most of my weekend chores. Mrs. Sloan insisted upon taking full responsibility for keeping our rooms clean—including making the bed each morning—so that left me with even more idle time. There were always letters to answer, for I corresponded with several friends and faithfully wrote to my family at least once a week, and there were books by current authors to be read because I was subscribing to one of Portland's rental libraries. However, I often grew tired of reading and then roamed around the house craving excitement.

Once in a while, though, I went with the other boarders to a Saturday night dance in Stanfield where most of the men who attended were middle-aged and married, so the occasions were not the answer to a single girl's prayer. Even so, they were wholesome affairs and an excuse to dress up and mingle with people, so I went whenever I had the opportunity.

The dances were of no great importance in my life, so I remember little about most of them, but I do remember the ride home from one I attended in Umatilla. Although the town is only fourteen miles from Stanfield, it took us more than two hours to get home, partly due to the fact that Vernon chose a winding, snow-covered trail through the desert instead of going directly home via U.S. Highway 30.

Last night Sue and Vernon took me with them to a big Masonic dance in Umatilla. The Shrine Band came up from Portland, so the music was an inspiration after the bang-bang orchestras of these parts. Vernon took his sister and a couple whom we knew to the dance also. The man and Vernon (who generally doesn't drink) bought a bottle of moonshine and had just enough so they were truly silly. They were like a couple of adolescent schoolgirls with the giggles. Everything was just too *good* (they thought).

Although it was uncomfortable to sit and watch

their antics as they got out of the car to watch the
moon with the thermometer about twelve degrees
above, it was amusing too. Sue was too disgusted
for words, besides being frozen, poor dear,
because she sat between them in the front seat and
they'd leave the car door open every time they got
out to look at the moon.

The radiator froze up as we rode along (or
maybe it was because they'd stopped) so they got
in and out, and out and in, trying to get thawed.

Finally, Vernon began to recite poetry—
everything from Wordsworth's "Daffodils" to
"The Owl and the Pussycat." But at least he
drove right on after that and didn't stop every few
miles to look at the moon.

The next day Vernon failed to show up for his usual Sunday
afternoon date with Sue. He customarily arrived just after our mid-
afternoon Sunday dinner and then took Sue out for the rest of the
day and evening. This time he stayed home all day.

When he finally made his appearance at seven p.m., he did not
stand around the kitchen or dining room visiting with the Sloans as
he generally did. Instead, he marched on into the seldom used
living room, with Sue trailing behind.

Tonight Vernon came up to the house to make
peace—only he's clever. He put Sue and me in the
wrong so we couldn't blame him. First, he insisted
that I come into the living room and be present
while he talked to Sue. Then he began by asking if
we had anything to say regarding the dance. While
we were trying to decide what to say, he continued
on, demanding to know if anyone had been
ungentlemanly.

We had to admit that he'd been polite and
refined acting, so he then went on to say that, as
far as he was concerned, he had had a good time,
etc., etc. Really he was quite eloquent—had Sue
and me feeling like self-righteous killjoys.

When I left the living room that evening, I had learned this
lesson: that sometimes the best way to defend oneself is to be the
first to attack.

One part of my weekend was always taken care of. If I were in town on Sunday morning, as I was most of the time, I was sure to be teaching Sunday School in the Presbyterian Church. In my letter of application to the Stanfield School Board I had given the required information about my height, weight, age, condition of health, etc., and stated that I was a Protestant, which probably influenced the Board's decision to hire me. Stanfield was a predominantly Protestant town so I doubt very much that they would have hired a Catholic teacher (and conversely in 1928, the school board of a predominantly Catholic town would not have been likely to hire a Protestant).

All nine teachers in the Stanfield schools were Protestant, and all were expected to support the town's one dominant church. There was another church which had a more emotional approach to religion, with a congregation that was largely composed of the less prosperous people in the community, but it was taken for granted that we teachers would not go there.

When I went to church the day after my arrival in town, I discovered that supporting the church meant much more than merely going to listen to the minister's sermon and putting money in the collection plate. After the services I was introduced to Mrs. Gibson, the minister's wife, and soon heard myself agreeing to teach a Sunday School class of eight and nine-year-old boys. On our way home Sue announced that she had been assigned a class of high school age youngsters. Gertrude had sung in the choir that morning—carrying on from the years before—and, beginning the next week, Margaret was to play the piano for Sunday School and church services.

On the following Sunday I looked around and saw that the girls who taught with Gertrude in the grade school building had also been pressed into service as Sunday School teachers. Then I observed Mr. and Mrs. Kelty and young Mrs. Woodhouse, the high school science teacher's wife, doing their bit by attending the Sunday School's Adult Bible Class.

Later on during the church services, I saw Wayne, my fellow Junior High Teacher, singing in the choir along with some of the faculty members who shortly before had been conducting Sunday School class. Yes, we were all present and doing our duty.

All this sounds very arbitrary because we were drafted to serve instead of being gently influenced to volunteer, but it was not too bad. It was good for public relations, of course, and through our church activities we met well-educated, interesting people from the countryside that we never would have known otherwise. Then, too, going to church dressed in our Sunday best was a welcome diversion and, of course, we could not ignore the beneficial effects of Mr. Gibson's sermon.

Not all of my weekends were spent in Stanfield. Sometimes I went to Pendleton, about thirty miles away and the largest town in that part of the state, to visit Mable Tacheron, one of my best friends from high school days. She and her husband Frank, had just recently moved there from Portland and since her two young sons—one an infant in arms—kept her close to home, she looked forward to my coming. I was as eager to see the "city" sights and browse through the shops as I was to renew our long-time friendship so I went as often as I could afford the extra expense of the bus fare.

Most of the time when I was there, evenings were spent quietly at home with Mable and Frank, but one time there was an exception to this rule.

Friday after school, I rode to Pendleton with Mr. Sloan so managed to drop in on Mable early. Later, I went with Frank, Mable, and some of their friends to see Al Jolson in *The Singin' Fool.* It was the first show I've seen in which the actors talk. Of course, the vitaphone has been "in" a couple of years, but it only produced stunts, songs, etc.

This *Singin' Fool* has been thoroughly discussed here at the house because Mr. Sloan, Margaret, and Gertrude had gone to see it too. I did enjoy it so much. Al Jolson is a superb actor.

After our party left the movie, we returned to Tacherons' house full of wonder at the remarkable invention which enabled us to hear movie actors speak their parts. We were so excited by the experience that we relived the whole show, discussing every little detail. Little did we dream that night what the future held in the way of entertainment. We could not know that an even more remarkable invention would make it possible for us to see and hear people talk to us from across the ocean or even from the moon while we sat in our living room.

When basketball season opened, I attended the home games and began to understand that the sport was of vital importance to the community because it was about the only source of entertainment during the winter. In spite of zero weather, home games were played before a crowd of cheering fans, who also braved long, cold trips to the teams' out-of-town games. I went along on these trips whenever I could get a ride. My diary tells of one of the times I went with Ike and Elizabeth Woodhouse, Stanfield's basketball coach and his wife.

> Last night Stanfield played Pilot Rock so we had to journey to Pilot Rock—45 miles from here. I didn't have to go, but craving something to do above all else, I begged a ride with the Woodhouses. They have a Ford roadster, so when we hit a blizzard, we felt the full blast.

> When I came stumbling into the house after the trip, Margaret was just getting ready for bed, and she thought it quite amusing to see the snow drifts on my hat and coat. The car robe we had over our laps in the roadster was heavily laden with snow, but even so, we didn't suffer much from the cold.

> There were five other cars from here. All of them, except the car Sue was in and the one Mr. Hoskins drove, had some kind of trouble. Some froze, and one even burst a differential (whatever that is).

> Between Pilot Rock and Pendleton we were hailed by a couple of young men whose car had frozen up dead. They left it and climbed upon the back of our car, riding outside that way until they couldn't stand the cold anymore. Then they sprinted into town. That's the excitement for this weekend.

Weekends were uneventful and utterly boring for the most part, broken only by Saturday night basketball games during basketball season and Sunday School classes and church services every Sunday. Sometimes there were more weekday activities to go to than on weekends but even these were hardly exciting.

> Last week every evening was full (after a fashion): Monday P.T.A.; Tuesday, a basketball

game; Wednesday, Sunday School teachers' meeting; Thursday, choir practice; Friday, another P.T.A. meeting; Saturday, up at Pilot Rock to see Rachel Sloan in a town play.

4

Life was consistently more interesting on school days, however, because I enjoyed my hours in the classroom and evenings passed quickly.

We boarders congregated in the big kitchen before dinner time, chatting and joking with each other or Mrs. Sloan as she prepared dinner. This meal was served some time after six o'clock because it gave Mrs. Sloan a longer work-free period in the afternoon, which she needed because Sue, Margaret and I came home for lunch most of the time. After lunch, she went shopping or attended bridge-club parties that sometimes lasted late into the afternoon. I remember that we were always ravenously hungry when we gathered around the table, and that I could never decide whether the food tasted so delicious because our landlady was such a good cook or because it had been so long since our last meal.

After dinner, when the wood fire died down in the kitchen range, we moved into the central hall and gathered around the floor furnace to talk, or if one of us had an interesting book, she went to her room to read it, lying on the bed.

I hoped to be a pianist someday so during the previous summer I had purchased a second-hand piano for $150.00 on the installment plan of fifteen dollars per month. After Christmas I began to take piano lessons from Mrs. Harry Rees, one of the people I enjoyed most in Stanfield. This interest in the piano developed after I had seen how important it was for an elementary teacher to be able to play one. Many times that was the difference between being hired or not being hired to teach in a school.

"The Merry Group on the Hill," Mrs. Sloan's boarders. Left to right in front row: Gertrude Lawrence, Sue Shepherd, Margaret Templer. Standing behind, Grace Brandt.

My fellow boarders did not appreciate it when I arose at 6:45 a.m. to practice, so I had to postpone playing my simple exercises until evening. At first my musical efforts seemed to be as amusing to the other girls as my practicing pivots for basketball coaching had been. They good naturedly followed me into the living room to acclaim my playing, but the novelty soon wore off, and I was left alone with my labors.

I generally could play the week's assignment almost perfectly when Mrs. Rees came to the house for my piano lesson, so she decided that I must be talented. In reality I was merely playing by ear. I always had been able to learn a tune quickly so when she helped me with the next week's lesson by playing the little melody, I memorized it and as I practiced, I unconsciously looked for the keys that would give me the tune instead of reading the notes. So I did not learn as much about music as I should have that winter.

The following year I discontinued the lessons because a heavier teaching load left me without time or energy to practice. So, to the end of my teaching career, I was never able to answer affirmatively that space on my application form which inquired if I could play an instrument. As for the piano which I had purchased so hopefully, I saw to it that my younger sister Clarice took lessons on it, so she would be better prepared for a teaching career than I had been.

I must admit that our extraordinarily satisfactory boarding place did lack a spare bedroom, so when one of us had an overnight guest, our roommate was expected to relinquish her half of the bed and go spend the night elsewhere. On two occasions—when my friend Verna Stark spent the night at Sloans, and later when my mother was there two nights—Gertrude stayed with Carl's sisters, but when Gertrude's mother came, I was not well enough acquainted with anyone in town to ask for a night's lodging.

I hinted that there might be enough room for the three of us in Margaret's and Sue's bed (since we were all slender) but they did not take to the idea. Finally, Mrs. Sloan arranged for me to stay with her friend, Mrs. Greathouse. Friday night Sue went with me, so I would not have to stay in a strange place alone, but due to my misunderstanding (or failure to ask) as to where Gertrude's mother planned to spend the following night, I did not reserve the room for a second time. Saturday I arrived home at 11:30 p.m. from an out-of-town basketball game and found Gertrude and her mother preparing for bed. I didn't have the nerve to disturb Mrs. Greathouse, and I didn't have enough money to go to the hotel. Also there was no invitation from Margaret and Sue to share their bed, so I saw no alternative but to sleep in my customary place.

Since our bedsprings were old, the bed sagged to the middle like a hammock, especially after Gertrude, who was quite heavy, climbed in. All year Gertrude had been putting a feather pillow in the middle every night to keep us from rolling together. It was into this sleeping accommodation—minus the pillow in the middle—that I crawled to join Gertrude and her mother. Needless to say, we all spent an utterly miserable night.

The next week I confided in my diary, using mixed metaphors to show how completely I had been debarred from Gertrude's favor:

> Gertrude hasn't spoken to me since Saturday but pointedly talks to other members of the family about the uselessness of being unselfish. I *know* that I should have done something about finding another place to sleep, but I failed to, so now I'm in a dark cloud with my head under a bushel basket.

But there were happier times. We gave a surprise birthday party for Sue which was a success because she was really surprised. And my twenty-second birthday did not pass unnoticed by those around me.

> Friday, 9:30 p.m.
> November 10, 1928
>
> Tomorrow's my birthday. I don't know why a birthday always thrills me, but it never fails to. I don't get many presents, generally, so it may be that it's just because I'm young enough yet to enjoy that special day.
>
> This birthday promises to be quite diverting. Tonight at the dinner table Mrs. Sloan and Margaret brought out their presents for me early as I'm going to Pendleton tomorrow. Mrs. Sloan gave me a bottle of ink in a clever little metal container and Margaret gave me a bath towel with "Best wishes for many baths" on her card. Gertrude came home from Pendleton while we were eating, and when she saw that the presents had been given, added three lovely embroidered linen handkerchiefs. They are by far the prettiest I've ever had.
>
> Mrs. Sloan had made me a lovely birthday cake which she let me cut, so I felt indeed like the guest of honor.
>
> At school the seventh and eighth grade girls gave me a handkerchief shower. They were all so happy about it.
>
> Any minute now Verna is due to arrive from Portland. She'll probably spend the night here, and then we shall drive on to Pendleton tomorrow morning to spend Saturday and part of Sunday with Mable.

Verna Stark and I came from the same neighborhood on the outskirts of Portland and as we grew up and saw our girl friends marrying and settling down, we joined forces. We were the old maids (aged 22 and 24) but we were free to go off on jaunts such as the one the previous summer to Victoria, British Columbia, with Verna at the wheel of her new 1928 Chevrolet coupe.

As I told the others in Sloan's household of my weekend plans to go to Pendleton with my friend, I could not resist the temptation to brag about her good-paying secretarial job ($1,800 per year when the average stenographer made closer to $1,200) or that she had bought her car out of her own earnings. It was even rather remarkable that she had driven it all the way from Long Beach, Washington, to Port Townsend, Washington, along Highway 101 when the highway was still in the first stages of construction. In many places we had traveled on dirt-surfaced roadbeds cut through the virgin forest. With only four months' driving experience she made the trip to Canada without mishap in those days when most women did not know the first thing about driving. I was proud of my best friend.

5

The bad weather furnishes much excitement and is a topic of conversation. It was sixteen degrees below zero here one night last week, but for the most part hovers around twenty degrees above during the day. The snow is about six inches deep.

I'm getting quite conceited, though, since I'm not noticing the cold to any extent at all. I think that is probably because Sloans have been keeping a fire in the furnace day and night, and if a person is thoroughly warmed-through in the house, then it's not so bad when he goes outside.

February 11, 1929

The weather is still cutting capers, skitting down to twenty-five degrees below zero. Still, I can hardly believe it is so cold, because we aren't bothered as long as our furnace is going full blast. At school the furnace furnishes plenty of heat because Mr. Greathouse, the janitor, stays at school day and night to stoke it with wood.

However, to get to the softness of our life—we've had no school for two days so far this week, and the School Board has closed school until the weather breaks because the buses had a hard time getting started. Wayne, who drives a bus from out in the country, didn't get to school until eleven a.m. the last day we taught, and one of the buses didn't ever get to school that day. The oil freezes up, they say, so it is absolutely impossible to get them to go. The board members are afraid they might stall on the road and put the children in danger of freezing.

Since this is lambing season, Mr. Sloan is pretty discouraged. Because of this bitter cold he is losing a great many lambs.

March 3, 1929

I must record our happenings of the past month. It was a sad day when the Board decided to close school on account of the cold, for we are now having a struggle to decide whether we have to make it up without pay or not. The Board hasn't done much struggling, for it has coyly kept our paychecks, and now that we've gone five weeks without pay, they still delay. At present I have only seventy-nine cents in the bank and owe a couple of dollars for some cash I've borrowed.

The members of the school board were really not as bad as I judged them to be, because they were deeply involved in the problem of school finances. The district was in debt for the fine high school building, so the board members had that to worry about as well as how to meet current expenses. The town bank had gone bankrupt a year or so before with a devastating effect in many instances. I remember hearing Mr. Sloan speak of ranchers' taxes

25

being delinquent, so the cummunity even then, in 1928, was going through hard times.

When they met to discuss school closures due to bad weather and attendant problems, they were also trying to decide what to do about rehiring teachers. Early in January Mrs. Sloan told me that, most likely, there would not be two teachers for the junior high grades next year. I knew that her information was reliable, for its source was Mr. Hoskins, who being Mr. Sloan's bosom friend, gave him detailed accounts of what occurred at the school board meetings.

Due to families moving out of the district, I had only thirteen pupils in my room, so I had to admit that combining the two grades was the logical thing to do. Since Wayne had been teaching in Stanfield longer than I, and was a favorite of Mr. Hoskins, and could coach, there was little doubt in my mind as to which one of us would stay. This meant looking for another teaching position, a prospect I dreaded but intended to face with great determination.

Oh, how I hate the stress and turmoil of making applications! I don't even know where I want to apply but I'm going to work like an office dog in a sweat-shop so I'll get a good recommendation. Then, too, I'll continue with my piano lessons and attend summer school so I can get a worthwhile teaching position.

March 3, 1929

We've heard that the Board is holding long conferences on what to do about reelecting Mr. Kelty. Since he's not terribly interested in basketball, some of the board members want to put him out. There's enough intrigue and scheming going on to furnish foundations for an international war.

March 11, 1929

Well, well. I'm here again and this time with the glad news that I've been rehired to the very same position I have now—one grade and that's all. Being on the lookout for easy positions, I've decided to sign on the dotted line the minute the contract is handed to me. I was surprised when Mrs. Sloan told me that I was the only teacher unanimously elected. Maybe I'm not *pleased!*.

Well, of course it was probably a mistake and someone forgot to object when he intended to. Next year, after I've been here two years, I shall seek a junior high school position in a bigger town.

March 25, 1929

One of the board members has resigned before we could all be ratified by the Board. We're in a rather precarious position—we're elected and yet we aren't.

April 5, 1929

At long last I have received word of the Board's *final* decision. They have decided to have the seventh and eighth grades under one teacher after all. Here it is April fifth and I've just been informed. They were big-hearted enough to offer it to me instead of Wayne, but I'm not thrilled about both grades with a total of from thirty to thirty-five pupils.

However, they are raising everyone's wages five dollars per month which amounts to fifty dollars per year. Tonight I went out on the school bus to see Mr. Hoskins about a hundred dollar raise which would bring me up even with Gertrude and the first grade teacher. That, incidently, would raise my salary up to $1,300—$144 per month for nine months. *That* would be hard to turn down.

But I don't actually believe that I'll get the raise. Gertrude is out-of-sorts with me because she knows I went out in the country some place along Wayne's bus route, but she doesn't know where. She'll find out anyway, so I don't know why I'm being so ornery and making such a mystery of it all. Still, Gertrude would be very upset if she knew I was out there trying to get my salary increased.

My contract called for an annual salary of $1,250.00 instead of the $1,300 that I had hoped for, but I knew that it was high compared to the average salary in western Oregon where teachers received two to three hundred dollars less per year. Appended to our contract was a note stating that "any days lost due to inclement weather during the ensuing school year will be made up *without pay."* And Mr. Kelty was rehired despite his lukewarm attitude toward athletics.

In choosing me to be their seventh and eighth grade teacher in spite of my failure as a basketball coach, the men on the school board did more for me than they would ever know. After that, whenever I was about to be overwhelmed by self-doubts, I would think of their vote of confidence and be reassured. In retrospect, I realize that the year's happenings brought a definite break-through in my struggle to attain self-assurance.

It was near the end of the school year—almost time for the state examination in geography—which made me feel worried because of the days lost during the cold spell.

March 11, 1929

We're going through Asia like a cold chill,
hardly even breathing between pages. I've decided
that we don't need to stop to ponder over the
habits of the Asiatics.

The middle-aged upper grade teacher in the neighboring town had the enviable reputation of practically never having a pupil of hers fail in the state examinations, so I was especially anxious for my class to be well-prepared. I thought this competition would make it doubly bad for me if my pupils made a poor showing, but by spring I had learned that there are many angles to the achievement of a reputation like my neighbor's. Thereafter I was less in awe of her impressive record.

This realization was brought home to me in January when a fifteen-year-old girl enrolled in my class after having been a pupil in the neighboring school district since the first grade. Now it had suddenly been discovered that she belonged in the Stanfield school district and could no longer legally attend her former school without paying tuition. I never did fully understand the legal basis for this maneuver, but by noon of the girl's first day in my room, I did understand why the neighboring teacher, who had a great deal of influence with her school board, wanted to push the pupil off onto me. She was well-behaved and tried hard, but it was evident that she was having trouble as far as geography was concerned so I had my doubts about her being able to pass the state examination.

In later experiences with testing in that area, I was further educated in the ways a teacher might protect her interests. The county school superintendent gave an advantage to veteran upper grade teachers in the county by inviting them to come to Pendleton to help grade the state examination papers.

28

My neighbor, who was one of the chosen few, was reputed to keep a close eye on anyone who was grading one of her pupil's test papers. If it appeared that the pupil would receive a failing grade, she rushed to the defense of his answer and in this way gained enough points to bring the grade up to a passing mark.

I had no such tricks, and I was lacking in influence to implement them even if I had known some, so all I could do was teach and drill my pupils in preparation for the examinations. However, I was sure that my pupils would do well. And they should have, because by that time I had only eleven pupils so I worked with them individually.

When I received the test grades from the county superintendent, they showed that *all* my pupils had passed the examination. I had been spared the probability of a failure when the slow-learning girl dropped out of school, as a pupil might when verging on sixteen.

The close of school was celebrated by having school picnics during the last week, and that was all, unlike Midland where the school year had ended in a blaze of glory.

> May 23, 1929
>
> Today was picnic day for all age levels in the school system. The grade school had a picnic down here in the park, and we took the junior high youngsters over to Echo on the Umatilla River. The high school people went farther away to Cold Springs on the Columbia River.
>
> Our picnic was a successful one for which I must give Wayne most of the credit. He's peppy and helps to make everyone have a good time at an affair like that.

Changes were in prospect, so life at our boarding place would be different the following year. Margaret had a contract to teach in western Oregon and Gertrude was being married to Carl that summer. As we rushed around preparing to leave town, we paused long enough to take proper notice of the impending break-up of the "merry group on the hill."

> Tomorrow all of the rest of us up here on the hill are giving Margaret a little farewell party. It really is a short reception since it will last from two-thirty to four o'clock but we haven't time to

have it last longer, because with packing, etc., we're terribly busy.

Tomorrow, I also have to put grades on the report cards, copy grades and averages on the permanent record cards, and finish balancing my register. However, most of the work in *that* is done.

As I looked back over my year in Stanfield that night, I summarized my impressions:

When one's teaching school, every year is one definite segment of time. This year hasn't been much to brag about because it has been so utterly devoid of social activities that I can't say I've been hilariously happy. There's always hope for the coming year, though.

Sue and I had half-heartedly talked about batching the next year in order to save money, but we didn't want to hurt Mrs. Sloan's feelings by looking for other places to stay. So when we left Stanfield, it was with the taken-for-granted understanding that we would board at the Sloans again when we returned in September.

6

During that year I always was down to my last dime by the end of the month even though I was earning more than I had at Midland. But of course, my expenditures were far greater now that I was paying thirty dollars for board, making payments on a piano, and reimbursing my parents for the cost of my first year at normal school. Bus and train fares for trips to Pendleton on weekends and to Portland at Christmas time, as well as buying Christmas presents, had also been a drain on my resources. Notwithstanding, out of an annual income of $1,200 I had managed to save $175.00 which would have to be doled out sparing since I intended to go to summer school. While still in Stanfield, I planned ahead by making a budget.

Tuition for summer school	$20
Room and Board at $1 per day	45
Lunches, carfare, and miscellaneous school expenses	30
Expenses not related to summer school	80

Once again back on my parents' farm near Gresham I began to go into Portland to look for a place to stay during the six week summer school session. Verna, who lived with her mother and stepfather, invited me to share her bedroom, but she recently had become engaged to be married so I knew she would be busy with her fiance. Instead, I arranged to live with Mr. and Mrs. Raleigh Lee, my sister-in-law's parents, even though they lived on the east side of the Willamette River, making it necessary for me to take a streetcar to downtown Portland and then transfer to another line in order to get to classes. Later on, I knew that my choice of a place to live had been a wise one, because it was in a quiet neighborhood and there were few distractions in the home to keep me from my studies.

Early in June I went to the Lincoln High School (now known as "Old Main" on the Portland State University campus) and registered for the University of Oregon's Extension Summer School. Opening day I met several girls I had known at Oregon Normal School, and during the following weeks I often joined one of them at noon to walk through the park blocks on our way to a downtown restaurant for lunch. At least once a week I met my friend, Verna, and spent the noon hour with her.

I was signed up for classes in Moral Education, Art for Elementary Teachers, and one in Magazine Writing which I dropped at the end of the first week when I learned that I would have to go around town looking for people to interview. The prospect frightened me, so I switched to a course in Medieval History.

The art class was taught by one of the art supervisors for Portland's elementary school system. She had just returned from a year of study in Vienna, Austria, where she had picked up the revolutionary idea that children should be encouraged to be artistically creative. Instead of merely coloring a picture the teacher had duplicated on the hectograph or having an art appreciation lesson, the pupil was to be shown how to express his originality. To provide the fundamentals for this type of teaching, our instructor taught us to draw trees, houses, animals and people and gave us practice in several other art activities, including handcrafts suitable for elementary school children.

I struggled by the hour during the afternoons and evenings, trying to produce a piece of work worthy to be handed in, because I was not naturally artistic and I had almost no previous art training. Although I earned an unimpressive "C" in the course, my time and efforts proved worthwhile, because of all the art classes I would ever take during a long teaching career, this one was the most helpful. Using this new method, I was able to teach art classes that were not only interesting but geared to each pupil's ability. I no longer had to feel apologetic about the bare appearance of my schoolroom, for there was always children's art on display, and what's more, it was interesting because every piece of work was different from the rest.

One day in July after Verna and I had lunched together, we browsed through the stores, talking incessantly because we had not seen each other for over a week and seemed to be overflowing with things to say to each other. Verna suggested that we meet again that evening and go to a movie, but I couldn't go because I was short of money and there was an art assignment to be finished.

Since I never had classes in the afternoon, I walked five blocks out of my way with her to the corner where she turned to go to her office. As we stood there on the corner still talking, Verna was shocked to see that she was already twenty minutes late and hurried away.

That evening I repeatedly drew and redrew in an effort to make my houses have the proper perspective when they were drawn at an angle. As I was having such a struggle, I decided that I might as well put the work aside and try again during the weekend. Then I called Verna to ask her if she still wanted to go to a show, but by that time she had promised to go with her stepbrother, Harry, for a ride on his motorcycle. Having nothing else to do, I went back to my art assignment and had it ready to hand in by the time I went to bed.

The next morning while I was enroute to my eight o'clock class, I was joined on the streetcar by a fellow summer school student who lived in Verna's neighborhood. She seemed to think that since we both knew Verna, there was a common bond between us. As she came up the aisle of the streetcar, I could see she was looking for me. She hurried to sit down beside me and asked if I had read the morning paper. When she learned that I hadn't, she blurted out the news she was bursting to tell me: Verna had been killed in a traffic accident the evening before.

"According to the paper," she rushed on almost enthusiastically, "one car tried to pass another and ran into the motorcycle Verna and Harry were on. Both of them were killed instantly."

I was in such a state of shock when I left the streetcar at the school stop that I could not go to class. Instead I boarded the next car going downtown and bought a paper at the first newsstand I came to, hoping that my informant had been mistaken. But it was all there in print just as she had said it was.

I boarded the streetcar that took me back to my boarding place and had just arrived there when the telephone rang. It was my mother calling from the farm where they had heard the news on the radio. She and my father were deeply concerned, not only because they had liked Verna, but because of the fact that this was my first experience with the death of someone I was close to. As I felt the loving compassion in her voice, I was grateful for the news that she and my father would soon be at Lees' to pick me up and take me back home with them.

Although Verna and her stepbrother, Harry Renne, had died Thursday evening, the memorial services were not held until the following Monday forenoon, so I stayed with my family until Sunday evening. Then I returned to town. As I sat in my bedroom the next morning waiting until it was time to dress for the funeral, I wrote in my diary. I filled pages recalling details of the last hours we spent together and then tried to express my feelings and also tell of plans for the funeral.

> This morning I feel peaceful about Verna. I feel as if she's just gone on ahead to another life where she can express all her fine qualities just as she has here. But in order to feel better about it, I *must* think there is a plan. Maybe she escaped some unhappy experiences here this way. It's not so bad—riding along full of pep and youth one minute and in another life the next.
>
> There will be a double funeral with girl pallbearers for Verna, but Harry's pallbearers will

lift and carry her casket for us. We girls are all
wearing light dresses which is better than a funeral
procession of men clad in funereal black.

I'm writing this before I go get dressed for the
funeral, because I'm afraid that afterwards I may
not be able to have faith that life is eternal.

I remember being in one of the rooms at the mortuary with the
other young pallbearers waiting to go out to take part in the
services. As I stood there feeling heavy-hearted, I noticed a small
picture on the wall beside me. It showed bright stars serenely
shining in a night sky, with this caption written below: "When we
love the stars so, why should we fear the night?"

For some reason, the question and picture reassured me, and I
felt comforted.

On August 27, six weeks later, I wrote:

It seems strange to me that I don't feel Verna's
death more keenly. We were awfully close and I
loved to be with her, yet I don't feel an aching
void the way I should have imagined I would. It
might be because I can't think of her as being
dead. At first I wouldn't let myself, because it
made me feel so bad, and now I always feel as if
she's merely away. I wish that I'd saved more of
her letters, since that is the way we shared our
serious thoughts. We were enough alike so we
understood each other's restlessness. I wrote to
her once a week these last two years, and she
answered me regularly.

It will be a long time, and maybe never, before I
find anyone with whom I feel so comfortable and
so sure of. I wish (and hope I *will*) learn from her
experience that it doesn't pay to worry and fret
and be rebellious, because we're here making
ourselves miserable about conditions one minute
and gone the next. As far as her personal problems of relationships, she should have gone ahead
and done what she wanted to do all along. She
might just as well have been married two years
ago.

Verna's death may not have left the aching void that I had read
about in books but nonetheless, I had one dream that periodically

came to me during the night for several years after that. In the dream, Verna was still alive and we were together talking and laughing just as we used to, and everything was all right again.

It is evident as I read through my diaries, that after my friend's death I had a more mature outlook. I was beginning to accept conditions as they were instead of fruitlessly longing for them to be more to my liking. Maybe I *did* learn from Verna's experience that sometimes life is short, so it "doesn't pay to worry and fret and be rebellious."

Verna Stark, with her younger brother, Robert Stark

All summer Sue and I had been exchanging letters and had finally decided to batch that winter. We needed to save for "worthy causes" such as Sue's sending her half-brother through college and my putting aside money on a regular basis, so I could go to college to earn my bachelor's degree.

We wrote to Stanfield making inquiries about housekeeping rooms and learned that two apartments were available, one in Mrs. Hill's home, and another on the second floor of the building that housed the pool hall and post office on the ground floor. Then Mrs. Sloan wrote that she would be willing to make a couple of rooms into batching quarters for us, so we ended up by agreeing to stay there. With light-housekeeping in mind I canned fruit and made jams and relishes to take back with me.

I had thirty-two dollars left out of the $175 with which I started the summer. I was determined to begin this school year unburdened by a big bill at Meier and Frank's department store, but even as I wrote of this determination, I owed the store twenty-eight dollars. There was no possible way that I could start the year unencumbered by debt, especially since I had to pay for my train fare to Stanfield and buy a new pair of shoes.

The latter was not an inexpensive expenditure. Even in those lower-priced times I paid between ten and fifteen dollars for shoes because my shoe size was a 9 AAAA, a size carried by only one or two large stores in the city. The longest women's shoes carried by most stores was an 8 and the widths ranged from C to EE, but nothing narrower. As a rule the average price was six dollars or less, but whenever *I* went to buy shoes, I had to pay twice that amount. Nevertheless, I ended my vacation on a cheerful note.

> This summer has had its ups and downs and more than its share of sadness, but thanks to summer school, it also had its bright spots.

> Although I rather dread the thought of another socially uneventful year in Stanfield, I'm keeping my fingers crossed that somehow it will be better this next year.

SECOND YEAR AT STANFIELD
1929-1930

Back at Stanfield
September 26, 1929

Almost three weeks I've been here, but my, oh my, how time flies! Batching and teaching twenty-eight youngsters in two grades hardly leaves time for breathing and no time to be bored. The first week the weather was *so* hot—over ninety degrees every day. Teaching was therefore a drag, so with getting accustomed to two grades and batching besides, I didn't have much hope for my survival. But now everything is lovely. It certainly must be true that if one is completely busy, there isn't time to be discontented, for I am living proof of that in my life this year, and therefore go around being happy about conditions in general.

I was living in the same house and same community, so it might seem questionable that I could have been so much more contented when I returned. But we were in a different set-up at the Sloans and I had been rehired and thereby given a vote of confidence by the school board, so I no longer was under a strain to prove my competence.

Our rooms up here at Sloans are by far the cutest rooms I've ever batched in. Compared to Summer Lake's and Midland's batching quarters, these rooms with their pretty new curtains seem like model rooms in a furniture store window.

Upon seeing them, Sue and I were surprised to see how successful Mrs. Sloan had been in converting the family dining room and an adjoining small bedroom into an attractive apartment. The big dining room table had been replaced with the brightly painted table and chair set with matching buffet that had formerly been in Sloans' breakfast nook. In one corner of our kitchen was a kerosene cookstove with a work table and shelves nearby. Since Mrs. Sloan's sink was next to the doorway between our apartment and her kitchen, we used the water from her faucets for cooking and washed our dishes in her sink.

On sunny days, of which there are so many in that part of Oregon, we could almost depend upon solar heat for warmth, because our apartment, located on the southeast corner of the house, was flooded with sunlight. There were two medium-sized windows in our bedroom and a large one in the dining room that we now used for a kitchen-sitting room.

However on gray days and evenings we depended upon Mrs. Sloan's wood cookstove or the heat trickling in from the floor furnace in the hall. This meant that the doors between our part of the house and Sloans' were never closed, so we were almost as much a part of their household as we had been the year before.

Now that we were cooking for ourselves, we were deluged with farm produce. Youngsters got off the morning school buses bringing paper bags and boxes full of vegetables and fruits until we hardly knew where to store it—either at school or after we took it to our apartment. In addition to students, there were others in the community who shared their bountiful crops with us, so one day when we arrived home from school, we found a bushel of tomatoes and another of grapes which a neighbor had left for us on Sloans' screened porch. I hadn't realized that so many garden crops could be grown out on the irrigation project until we began to receive cantaloupes, apples, peaches, potatoes, green peppers, sweet corn, "tomatoes and more tomatoes," and carrots as well as the less familiar offerings of eggplant and green figs.

When Vernon brought us venison steaks during hunting season, we could have truthfully said, "Our storage place runneth over."

Even though we did not feel isolated from the Sloans, our changed mode of living gave us an entity of our own as a separate unit within their household. When Sue was out with Vernon weekends and evenings, I now felt independent enough to look outside the house for companionship and amusement.

I found this in the home of Ike and Elizabeth Woodhouse with whom I had become friendly the previous year when they gave me rides to out-of-town basketball games. They had recently put a considerable amount of money into the purchase of a console radio, for by 1929-1930 radios had improved to the point where they were a reliable source of entertainment. Ike and Elizabeth were anxious to show off their new possession, so Ike invited me to come to dinner one night and I gladly accepted because I had been reading about the improvements in the radio. After that I went there quite often, sometimes meeting Mr. and Mrs. Kelty and their children who had dropped in for a visit. Although my diary mentions that I enjoyed the fine new radio, I don't recall the names of particular programs. But I do remember sharing the Woodhouse's Sunday evening meals and 1 also recall the time I helped Elizabeth tie the pieced quilt she had laboriously put together. But best of all, I remember that I was certain of a warm welcome whenever I showed up on their doorstep.

While Mr. Greathouse, the school janitor, was sweeping my floor one fall day after school, I learned that he and his wife were also proud owners of one of the new radios. When I first started to teach in Stanfield, Mr. Greathouse had won my heart by bringing a flower planter full of plants to brighten my room and later, during the bitter cold spells, had taken care to see that the plants didn't freeze. While we talked about his radio, he chuckled at the thought of an incident in the ''Amos 'n Andy'' program he had heard the night before and then made the suggestion that Sue and I come down to their place for the next episode. Both of us knew and liked his wife, the town telephone operator, so we felt free to take advantage of his offer. For the next several weeks until the weather became too stormy, we dropped everything in order to be at the Greathouses at 7:00 p.m. on the night when Amos and Andy came on the air. Carrying a flashlight, we trudged along a muddy shortcut into town for a quarter of a mile, and one time we even braved a light snowstorm in order to hear the conclusion of one segment of the ongoing story.

Whatever had been done to commemorate my twenty-second birthday the year before was surpassed by the celebrations for my twenty-third birthday.

On my birthday there was much excitement around Stanfield. Saturday night Mrs. Shake, the mother of one of my pupils, invited Sue Vernon, and me down to dinner. When we were seated, lo! an ornate birthday cake, with candles and all, decorated the center of the table, so I decided that I was guest of honor. Sunday, Sue and I cooked my birthday dinner and had Mrs. Sloan come in to help us eat it, so that was dinner number two.

The girls in my room did their part by unexpectedly showing up at Sloans during the forenoon on my birthday (November 11) which was always a holiday. When they invited me to go on a hike with them, I said I would. But first we stopped at the high school, and then it was plain to be seen that I was in for another meal in honor of my natal day--this time one that they themselves would cook in the home economics room.

I had lots of fun helping them fix the little luncheon they had planned for me. Later, while we were still at the table, they gave me some birthday presents: a pair of bronze bookends from Shooks' drugstore, which they all had chipped in to buy, and a nice little hardbound cookbook put out by the Royal Baking Powder Company. We ended up by going for a hike along the Umatilla River where Billy Hedrich gave a prepared talk about the bridge, its size, history, etc.

Because of the donors who had gone to so much trouble to plan the day, I was sentimentally attached to those birthday gifts for a long time. And I still use some of the recipes in the now-battered little cookbook.

I suppose that the reason we four teachers had seldom been invited out to dinner during the previous year was because we were considered to be a group and therefore must be treated alike. To avoid the considerable work of having all four of Mrs. Sloan's boarders people didn't ask any of us, excepting, of course, the frequent occasions when Sue and Gertrude ate with their beaux' relatives. The next year Sue and I received several dinner invitations. We stayed in Stanfield over Thanksgiving vacation, and the Kelty family did too, so Mr. and Mrs. Green who lived on a ranch invited all of us to share Thanksgiving dinner with them and their teen-age son and daughter, Stanley and Elaine.

And there were others who were equally kind. It seemed as

though the community accepted us as one of them now that we were doing our own housekeeping.

In the meantime school events were also a source of interest and satisfaction.

Nov. 3, 1929

The High School Carnival took place last Thursday. It was a huge success in every way. Our room made $18.10 in contrast to the $1.50 the two Junior High rooms made last year. We had the pie and cider booth with everything donated so it was clear profit. Eddie Attebury made the cider out of the apples furnished by several parents.

Florestine Kelty thought of making flapper dolls from braided crepe paper, so with Hedricks' house as headquarters the doll-making operations were underway. On their own initiative the boys and girls who live near enough came every evening and weekends until they had made 51 dolls.

I was proud of everyone in the room for being so responsible and working so hard to make our booth a big success. From the 26 pupils in our room we received 20 pies to sell. That's wonderful cooperation--in fact almost a miracle.

And beating the high cost-of-living could be another challenging interest.

This month Sue and I kept our expenses down to twenty-four dollars apiece. And next month we're aiming for twenty dollars apiece, but I don't know about our success since it seems to call for a lot of economizing. We've bought a hundred-pound sack of potatoes, ten gallons of kerosene (for our cookstove), and today the canned fruit I put up last summer arrived from home, so now we have fifty pints of home-canned jams, relishes, and fruits. Altogether, we ought to have a few things accumulated, but now we're running out of sugar, cocoa, etc., so *they* must be replaced. Such a worry!

Nonetheless, I was able to report during the second month of batching that we had kept living costs for each of us down to nineteen dollars. When we compared that amount to the thirty dollars per month we had formerly paid Mrs. Sloan for board and room, we were well pleased with our decision to batch.

Late in October of 1929, Mr. Sloan called our attention to the huge headlines in The Morning Oregonian which had to do with the financial crash on Wall Street. As he discussed the situation with us, I was sobered by his serious mien, for he was trying to make us realize that the whole country's economy might feel the effects of that crash.

In those days hard times were almost always accompanied by bank failures, and since I intended to have money accumulating in a savings account throughout the year, I was deeply concerned. I had heard Ike Woodhouse tell about the time, two years before this, when he became suspicious of the Stanfield bank's solvency. Acting upon this hunch, he withdrew the money he was saving to buy a car and kept it at home in a quart fruit jar. After that, when payday rolled around, he cashed his check and added some more savings to the several hundred dollars in his fruit jar. When the bank closed, as it did in a few months, those who had checking and savings accounts lost their money, but not Ike.

Now, as I mulled that story over in my mind, I was certain that I did not have Ike's gift for instinctive foreboding, so I fussed and worried.

> There's so much excitement on Wall Street now that I'm afraid to put my money in the savings account of the Pendleton bank for fear the bank will go broke. I can't quite decide what to do. First, I thought of Postal Savings, but that only pays 1½ per cent interest. Then I was advised to buy school warrants which pay six per cent, but the drawback there is that they are never "called for" in less than a year's time, so if I want to go to college next year, I would merely hold them and then be forced to sell them before they were due. That way I wouldn't earn interest on my money.

When I wrote of "warrants," I was referring to promissory notes issued by a school district in lieu of checks when there were insufficient funds in the district's bank account to meet its obligations. In normal times these notes, which paid six per cent interest, were considered a good investment by banks or other interested parties who bought them from the holder at face value. One of the banks in Pendleton regularly bought the Stanfield school district's warrants and continued to do so in 1929 during the months of October through December, but in January it changed its policy.

January 25, 1930

The big source of worry this year is that the school district's warrants are not salable. Due to the fact that the district is so far behind in its tax receipts, it can't buy up the warrants until two years after they are issued, and of course banks can't make an investment like that. We believe that the bank will probably buy this month's (January's) warrants, but what will happen after that is a big mystery. There are all kinds of conflicting opinions regarding the ability of the school board to find buyers for the warrants.

February 7, 1930

Last Friday (February first) was pay day but the bank in Pendleton that has been buying our warrants won't even consider taking them any more. The people in this community don't have extra money, so they can't help us out by buying the school warrants either, so here we sit, holding pieces of paper that can't be cashed.

Mr. Kelty held a faculty meeting last Friday and broke the news gently, but it wasn't gently enough. The girls who teach with Gertrude at the other school had expected to receive their money that day, so when they heard that none was available, tears began to flow. They had spent most of their savings for Christmas, so one of them, Mildred, has only sixteen dollars saved up which certainly isn't much, if it's all you have in the world.

We've been rushing around frantically trying to see some way out. We don't know yet, but we believe we can *borrow* on the warrants, paying the banks eight per cent interest to loan us money on them. When we get the money from the district, they will pay us only six per cent interest, so we'd lose two per cent on the deal, but at least it would be something coming in.

Mr. Kelty understood that the school board had told him to close school if we could not manage to go on. We took a vote, though, and decided to carry on for three weeks to see what the school board can do in the meantime and then see whether to continue teaching for the rest of the year or not. The idea was to get the people riled up a bit, so they would be interested. The youngsters were all excited. It wasn't a very fair thing to threaten to close that way, but I don't see that it should be entirely our problem.

When I said that we'd been rushing around "frantically," that was the literal truth. One afternoon after school, five of us crowded into Ike's little Model T roadster--two on the running boards and three of us inside--to go to the home of an elderly couple out on the irrigation project who were reputed to have money to invest. Naturally we hoped to interest them in buying up school warrants, but they backed away from our proposition, assuring us that they were not as wealthy as people thought they were.

On our way back to town, someone thought of an elderly woman, a fellow church member, who gave the impression of being well-to-do (or maybe it was because we had heard a rumor that she had a wealthy son on the east coast), but anyway, Ike headed the roadster in the direction of her home. As we crowded into her living room, we could see that she was overwhelmed by this visitation from so many of us. In order not to appear too abrupt, one of us made a comment about the handsome children in pictures around the room. It developed that they were of her beloved grandchildren, so we were subjected to a long discourse about each one. When we finally were able to introduce the subject of warrants, we learned that she too, was not interested in the investment.

The only good that came from our rushing around, we decided afterwards, was that we had given a lonesome old lady a chance to talk about her grandchildren. We also were convinced that most of the local people didn't have money to invest, and if they did, it was not likely that they would use it to buy school warrants.

February 18, 1930

We've found out for sure that we can't *borrow*
on our warrants, so affairs are in a worse state
than ever. We've become so accutomed to having
no money, though, that it doesn't even interest us
now. I drew my two hundred dollars out of the
savings account and sadly said goodbye to all my
dreams of going to college next year. But I'll have
around seven hundred dollars out on interest as a
result of this year's experience.

The owners of the general merchandise store, Mr. and Mrs.
Refvem, came to the teachers' rescue by offering to accept warrants
in exchange for groceries. This was not so badly needed by Sue and
me (who had savings) as it was by some of the others. But it met
the needs for groceries of every teacher on the staff, because
everyone of us was either married or batching. To make it more
convenient for us to give warrants in exchange for groceries, the
school clerk occasionally made out several small warrants in our
name which had the total value of one month's pay.

The district was in such desperate financial straits that its board
members appealed to the county and state school officials for
advice. One day the Umatilla County School Superintendent came
from Pendleton and the Oregon State Superintendent of Public
Instruction from Salem to meet with the local board, hoping to find
a solution to our money problems. The reason that I remember
their visit so clearly is because Mr. Kelty brought the two
superintendents and the local board members in to watch me teach.
I suppose they were making the rounds of all the teachers' rooms,
since they were sure they could do *that* even if they could not
discover any answer to our monetary dilemma.

By then, I had taught long enough so it did not upset me when
the dignitaries came into the room. This was partly due to the fact
that I had trained my pupils to be especially courteous and
well-behaved when we had guests. That day, however, I was
embarrassed during the seventh grade language class when one of
the boys went to the front and read a business letter he had written
for that day's assignment. It was a letter of complaint to a laundry
in which he indignantly wrote that, instead of the dozen
handkerchiefs he had sent to be laundered, a dozen diapers had
been delivered to his door.

When I heard him repeatedly use the word "diaper" in front of our visitors, I was flustered because in those days of strict censorship and careful regard for proper language it seemed rather coarse to have that word used so openly. I was afraid they might think that I did not enforce strict enough discipline.

There were rumors, and rumors of rumors throughout the year, so we were constantly in a state of emotional tumult. At one time, early in April, we heard that from then on we would not be able to cash any more warrants, but in the end, I was forced to hold only $250 worth of the district's notes which were redeemed two years later at a value of $282.00.

2

Beyond a doubt, much of my attention that year was focused upon finances, but life went on whether or not warrants were cashed, and then too, the weather was such that it could not be ignored. All over the state in 1930, it was an unusually severe winter. In letters from home I learned of icy winds and deep snow in that ordinarily more temperate part of Oregon. Snowdrifts closed the roads to automobile traffic, making it impossible for the mailman to make his rounds, so in order to get the mail my brother hitched one of the plow horses to a farm sled and went to the post office in Boring by that means. And in Stanfield, as we played cards during the evenings, we huddled close to the floor furnace, because the weather that winter was even colder that it had been the year before.

January 25, 1930
Just as one year ago we were exclaiming over the weather, so we are today, and have been for the past week or so. It was thirty degrees below zero one morning and has been twenty degrees below every evening for a week.

Stanfield, profiting by last year's example, has not closed the school, because if we do, we will have to make up the time in the spring. All the other schools up and down the highway for miles have closed, but not us.

By means of dressing for the cold, I manage to keep warm enough. I wear a pair of wool stockings, some short wool socks over them, and my hiking boots to school so at least my feet are warm. And by wearing many sweaters, petticoats, undershirts, and a wool dress, it doen't seem really disagreeable at all on the way to and from school.

I may not have suffered from the cold during the quarter mile walk, but even so, when I arrived at school one morning, I had a frost-bitten nose.

Several times during the cold spell I went with groups of high school students to slide down a sharp incline on one of the low hills out in the country. The youngsters rode out there in cars and farm trucks which also carried fuel for a bonfire, sleds and anything else—even coal shovels—that would carry a passenger downhill.

As soon as we arrived, some of the boys threw water that they had brought for that purpose down the incline to make an icy surface, while others hurried to build a bonfire on the top of the hill. I recall standing near the fire, enjoying the beauty of the bright moonlight glistening on the snow-covered landscape, as well as the thrill of a swift sled-ride. I also remember that the ride, which seemed to be over in less than a minute, was inevitably followed by a laborious climb back to the top dragging my vehicle.

As I write this, the thought occurs to me for the first time that, unknowingly, I might have been there in the role of a chaperone. Perhaps some parents objected to their young people being out in a group where no older person was present, so it may be that I was invited to go along because I was the only adult foolish enough to venture out into the cold that night. But I prefer to think that the teenagers had no ulterior motives and that I was included because they liked having me along.

Not long after Christmas, Rachel Sloan came home to spend the rest of the winter with her parents. We were about the same age, so I welcomed her presence in the house now that Sue was spending most of her free time visiting Vernon who was ill much of that winter.

47

However, when the thermometer was hovering at thirty to forty degrees below zero, Sue stayed close to home and then we three girls and Mrs. Sloan played auction bridge. As soon as she saw how poorly we played the game, Mrs. Sloan took it upon herself to make Sue and me into more challenging opponents. My greatest weakness as a card player was that I seldom had the courage to bid so Mrs. Sloan made it the rule that regardless of the cards we held, each of us had to take the bid in rotation. When it was my turn I was surprised to see that I could win most of the time even if I didn't have every high card in the deck.

My courage was temporary, however, and did not sustain me later at a community card party where I was confronted by elderly, deadly serious card-playing members of the Ladies' Bridge Club. Even to have one as a partner was intimidating. After a couple of plays around the table, not only my partner but both opponents seemed to know exactly what cards I held, and I sensed that they seldom approved of what I did with them. Mrs. Sloan had done her best to make me into a card player, but I lacked an intuitive card sense as well as the killer instinct displayed by my bridge-playing adversaries. Maybe she had better success with Sue, but about that I have no recollections.

When the cold spell finally came to an end, some of the townspeople were inspired to organize a party to celebrate the return to normal temperatures. All adults were welcome to attend and were asked to bring cake and sandwiches. Cardplaying enthusiasts, of whom Stanfield had a goodly number, were asked to furnish card tables and cards.

When it was time for the party, Mrs. Sloan, Rachel, and I walked downtown to the vacant store where the party was to be held. Mrs. Sloan immediately sought out her bridge-playing cronies, while Rachel and I joined in some lively party games and then square danced—which I considered "great fun"—and like many others, I visited with friends whom I had not seen since the onslaught of the bitter cold. Later when refreshments were being laid out on tables, Mrs. Sloan, Rachel, and I left because we hadn't brought food to the party.

Because the get-together was such a huge success, everyone agreed that we should do it again. But it had been a spontaneously joyful reaction to the return of normal temperatures which made it possible to go out in comfort again, and this spontaneity could not be duplicated. So Stanfield resumed its rather unsociable state of mind in which lively community parties did not flourish.

According to reports from reliable sources even greater austerity would be the rule for Stanfield's schools the next year. Elementary teachers' salaries would be cut to $900 (almost a 25% cut), only two teachers would remain on the high school staff, no married teachers would be reelected, (this applied to Gertrude), and all the grades, one through high school, would be housed in the high school building. When we heard of all the proposed changes, most of the faculty began looking for positions elsewhere.

February 18, 1930

For the first time in my career as a teacher, I'm signed up for a school in February. Of course, it's just a "trick" job but I'm signed up just the same.

It is this way: Rachel and I, by perusing the register of teachers (and their salaries) put out by the county school superintendent's office, discovered that the two room school at Meacham pays the principal *fifteen hundred dollars!* and $1,260 to the lower grade teacher. That figure, $1,500, dazzled my imagination just as the thought of the Seven Cities of Gold must have fascinated the Spanish explorer, Coronado. I couldn't forget it, so when I saw that Rachel also was interested, we made up our minds to go there and apply for the position the following Saturday. We hired the Martin boy across the road from Sloans to drive Sloans' car, and with Mrs. Sloan to act as manager we started out.

All the way from here to Pendleton there were merely patches of snow on the ground, but after we left the lower elevation around Pendleton and started up into the Blue Mountains, we began to see more and more snow. By the time we reached Meacham, which is at the summit, we felt as if we were in the midst of winter again.

After we arrived, we had quite a time finding out about school board members, etc. We asked at the store, which is about the only thing there besides a few houses, and learned where the clerk of the school district lived. When we found her, she said that there were two other applicants in town, a middle-aged man and wife, and that the Board had about decided to hire them.

"In fact," she informed us, "the board members are going to meet with them in a few minutes, and most likely they will give them contracts."

Since it looked as if we had arrived too late, we didn't know what to do next so we stood in the clerk's living room discussing the matter. Her Swedish husband, (who was all in our favor) kept urging us to go ahead and put in our application anyway, exclaiming from time to time with a strong Swedish accent, "I would take no chances. I would take no chances!"

Then Mrs. Sloan reminded Rachel and me that Mr. Sloan had advised us to make a special effort to see one of the board members named Mr. Baker and let him know that Rachel was his (Mr. Sloan's) daughter. He had thought that might put us on the inside track because he and Mr. Baker were both Masons.

We went looking for Mr. Baker and discovered that he had just arrived after riding horseback from his ranch nine miles back in the mountains. As soon as he learned that we brought greetings from Frank Sloan and that Rachel Sloan wanted to teach in Meacham, the job was ours as far as Mr. Baker was concerned. For all he knew, we couldn't even read and write, but that apparently was relatively unimportant compared to the fact that one of us was the daughter of a highly respected member of the Masonic Lodge.

He told us that he would meet us later at the grocery store's lunch counter, adding that if "these other people" weren't satisfactory, we'd be considered next. As he left us, we all were pretty sure that he wouldn't find them satisfactory.

We were parked right in front of the store entrance so from our ringside seat we were able to see our rivals come banging out of the store (where the school board met) spluttering about the latest

"arrivals" in town. Anyway, after meeting with
the Board we were given contracts, but what
sinking feeling it gave us to hear them say that the
wages had been reduced to $1,200 for me and only
$1,000 for Rachel.

The work is a joke, though, nine pupils in one
room and eleven in the other. A teacherage is
furnished free, so we could save much money.
Also, the railroad which runs through the entire
length of the district probably pays its taxes on
time, so the district's warrants could be cashed.

We are signed up but hope we can find
something better. Meacham is such a *primitive* little settlement—no sidewalks, houses unpainted,
and just the highway and railroad running
through for the high spots of interest. The snow
gets six feet deep because it's in the middle of the
Blue Mountains, and the temperature falls to fifty
degrees below zero. But it does give us a secure
feeling to know we can be sure of a job for next
year and one that pays almost as much as
Stanfield paid this year.

We signed the contracts and then with Mr. Baker leading the way
went to inspect the schoolhouse and nearby teacherage. The school
was a crude, two-room structure, and the teacherage was a small
unpainted building like most of the other houses in Meacham. But
upon hearing that school supplies were provided free of charge to
the pupils, I was truly impressed. Writing materials, pencils, pens,
ink, paste, as well as crayons and any art materials the teacher
might desire were provided by the district. But apparently there
was a limit to even this district's generosity for I heard Mr. Baker
making bitter complaints about the great amount of paste the
teacher had used that year.

I could not help but contrast Meacham's liberal spending habits
with the parsimony I was asked to practice at Stanfield where even
chalk was rationed out sparingly to be used only by the teacher.
When the weather was stormy, my pupils could not amuse
themselves during the noon hour by drawing or playing games on
the blackboard because that would waste the chalk. As for the art
supplies used in our room, I had purchased them with the money
we had taken in at the high school carnival.

51

On March 19th—a month later—the lady chairman of the Meacham School Board declared that our contracts were illegal because they had not been signed at a regular meeting. We suspected that she was not so much concerned about the contract's legality as she was about the fact that the other board members had hired us instead of the people whom she wanted. However, that was not the last of the matter, because our applications were still on file and in effect even though we had returned the ill-fated contracts. At the next formal board meeting they were considered again—at the instigation of Mr. Baker, no doubt—and we were hired according to the letter of the law. Rachel signed this second contract and taught there the following two years, but I held back and wrote in my diary, "I'm not too keen on Meacham."

There were several reasons why I was not "keen" about the position. Mostly because of the district's location and the wintertime cold, but there was also the possibility that I might be called upon to teach a couple of ninth graders. I was certified to teach through the ninth grade, but I doubted that I could do a good job of teaching algebra, which had been one of my weaker subjects when I was a high school freshman. As I considered the situation, I wondered if I might not be repeating the mistake I made when I foolishly agreed to coach the girls' basketball team at Stanfield.

In the meantime, even while I though my Meacham contract was legal, I had been industriously looking around for a more attractive position. Still longing to teach history in a bona fide junior high, I wrote to ask if there were openings in Baker, The Dalles, La Grande, or Pendleton. But just to be on the safe side, I also contacted my friend, Elizabeth Murray, school superintendent of Columbia County, who twice before had helped me find teaching positions—at Midland, a Columbia River island school in the Clatskanie school system, and here in Stanfield.

She promptly sent the names of some districts needing teachers, including Wilark, a logging camp. So I applied for the schools and then sat back and waited. The only encouragement I received from the town schools was a letter asking me to come to Pendleton for a personal interview with the city school superintendent which might had led to a contract, but by then I had received a telegram from Wilark.

The telegram stated that I had been hired to be principal of their two-room school for a nine-months term at $140 per month, or $1,260 per year—the highest salary I had ever received. Although teaching in a two-room school again was a step downward professionally, I didn't hesitate to send the clerk an acceptance letter. The pay was high, and living expenses would probably be lower than in a town, making it easier to save money for college— and that outweighed all other considerations.

In a few days I received a contract and a note with the information that free firewood and a rent-free teacherage were also provided. That increased the annual value received by another $100. During those times when a cutback in teachers' salaries was a common practice, the generosity of the Wilark School District seemed too good to be true.

During the following year I realized that I had reason to be grateful when the clerk of the Wilark School District told me that there had been almost one hundred applicants for the principalship at Wilark which was one of the highest paid elementary teaching positions in Columbia County. I knew that once again I was indebted to Elizabeth Murray, for she had written to me about the vacancy, and then gone out of her way to recommend me to the school board.

With the following year's employment taken care of, I could breathe easier and attend to the duties related to the closing weeks of school. These included the final reviews for the state tests, administering the tests, completing school records for the year, and supervising the last day of school picnic.

As I prepared to leave, I looked in retrospect at my two years' stay.

> I can't say that I feel heartbroken about leaving Stanfield, although it has been an agreeable little town. As I've reiterated in these pages many times, the town is not thrilling at all—not a place to which one would look back with nostalgic longing. Without a doubt, knowing and living with the Sloans has been one of the best parts of the whole experience. Otherwise, these two years were just neutral in interest mostly because there aren't many young unmarried adults around here.
>
> I suppose, though, that I might just as well learn now as ever, that life isn't one grand everlasting song and dance.

Stanfield school system's teaching staff, 1929-1930. Left to right: Helen Sande [Margaret Templer's replacement], Sue Shepherd [high school], Leora Devin [first and second grades], Mr. William Kelty [superintendent], Grace Brandt [grades 7 and 8], Ike Woodhouse [high school], Mildred Bush [grades 3 and 4], Gertrude Lawrence [grades 5 and 6].

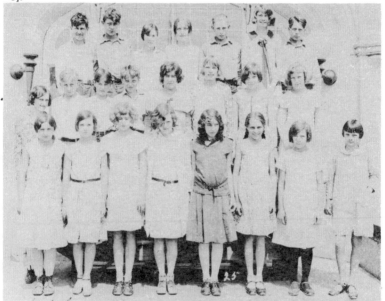

Stanfield Junior High students, 1929-1930. Bottom row, left to right: Lafeda Nudo, Idamae Isensee, Edna Lay, Julia Colpitts, Ardelia Herley, Bytha Hoskins, Cleo Green, Marie Thorsen. Middle row: Grace Brandt, Raymond Attebury, Tom Laughry, Stanley Wessell, Anna Correa, Thelma Norquist, Donna Shake, Myrta Martin. Top Row: Sammy Nudo, ? ?, Viola Krause, Irene Attebury, Kenneth Lay, Wilhelmina Hedrick, Eddie Attebury.

My diary has no account of my last days in Stanfield or my taking leave of the people in the community. Whether they gave me a farewell party or merely waved as I went by to board the bus for home, I do not remember. However, I trust that we parted with a mutual feeling of good will.

Five of the eight teachers who taught at Stanfield that year found other teaching positions for the following year, but Sue decided to continue to teach there despite the fact that she and Mr. Kelty would be the only teachers in the high school. She taught for two more years before marrying Vernon and then spent two or three years on a farm on the reclamation project before returning to teaching. For many years before her retirement, she was a junior high counselor in the Parkrose schools near Portland where she and Vernon still live.

Through Sue and Vernon, who frequently visit relatives in the Stanfield area, I kept track of the Sloans better than I would have if I had depended solely upon the annual letter I received from Mrs. Sloan at Christmas time. But now they are both gone. Mr. Sloan died several years ago, and Mrs. Sloan more recently after having lived more than ninety years.

Rachel Sloan married and had one son from whom both Mr. and Mrs. Sloan derived much pleasure since he spent a great deal of time with them. Rachel continued to teach schools close to Stanfield until she retired.

After leaving Stanfield, Ike Woodhouse taught in Baker, Oregon, but through failure to keep in touch my friendship with Ike and Elizabeth came to a close when we left Stanfield.

In 1978 my husband and I attended one of Stanfield High school's annual reunions. It marked the fiftieth anniversary of the class of 1928 and it was fifty years since I had first gone to Stanfield to teach.

We met in the old high school building, which was still in use, but additions, including a new gymnasium, had been made to the original structure. The area used for concrete tennis courts in 1928 was occupied by some kind of a school shop building.

It was fun to see and visit with Sue and Vernon Waid, the former Margaret Templer, and Rachel Sloan, as well as Leora Devin who had taught first grade when I was there. Another interest was talking with Wayne McGowan and several other people whom I had known as high school students.

The reunion was remarkably well attended by alumni from near and far but I was disappointed to see only three or four of my former pupils there.

One rather amusing highlight of the occasion, as far as I was concerned, was having a gentleman from Washington, D.C., whose name I have forgotten, approach me and declare that he'd always remembered me because I had gone to his rescue when he was an undersized high school freshman. He recalled that as soon as I learned a husky seventh grader was picking on him in the boys' restroom, I had bravely marched into the forbidden area and put a stop to the commotion.

Although I had no recollection of the incident, hearing about it made me realize that it is impossible to know just what will be stored away in a youngster's memory of his or her school days.

3

As a result of having been *forced* to be economical, I had money on hand or out on interest by the time the school year came to an end.

> June 1, 1930
> It certainly is a satisfactory feeling to have some money saved. I have loaned $100 to Johnny and am thinking of loaning fifty dollars to the folks, so with the $250 that the school district couldn't pay me I'll have $400 out on interest. Besides that, I have another $250 to spend this summer or do whatever else I want to with it.

Of the two choices that I gave myself, one implied that I might save the money, but I preferred to spend it, now that my plans to go to college had been disrupted. All spring I had been trying to think of something out-of-the-ordinary to do that summer.

June 30, 1930

Well, at last I've made up my mind about what
I'm going to do this summer. I've sent in my
money to reserve a place on the University of
Oregon Alaskan cruise in August. This way I can
earn nine hours of college credit and have a three-
week vacation at the same time. And I can afford
the $175 it will cost me.

Clothing styles were changing that summer, so dresses were form
fitting after being sacklike for years, and hemlines were plunging
from someplace around the knees to midcalf or lower. During the
1929-1930 school year I had little money to spend on clothes, so my
wardrobe (including an expensive coat with a fox collar that had
made me feel like a princess when I first wore it) was not only out
of style but beginning to show signs of wear. Now I had the excuse
that I was going on a cruise, so I went all out to bring my wardrobe
up to date.

July 22, 1930

Saturday I bought another dress. Honestly, I
don't know what ails me unless I'm doing this
buying because these new styles are designed for
tall women so are becoming to me. I've been
buying and *buying* clothes so now have four
dresses for which I've had little use this summer
out here on the farm.

But I really must report that a great change has
come into my life. With any other girl it would be
of a romantic nature, but with me it is that I am
becoming reconciled to being tall when I see
myself in these new-style form-fitting dresses.
They show off my figure so I look slender instead
of just thin.

When it was nearly time for the Alaskan cruise, I rode the train
to Eugene where an orientation week in preparation for the trip
was being held on the University of Oregon campus.

Sue, whose home was in Eugene, had written to ask me to stay
with her. If I did, it would save me the expense of living in a
dormitory and besides, I thought it would be fun to see Sue again.

However, that proved to be an unwise move, for I boarded the S.
S. Admiral Rogers in Seattle a week later without having become

well-acquainted with anyone else signed up for the cruise. I had attended classes and meetings during Orientation Week without making new friends because I always hurried back to Sue's place.

The schedule allowed for an entire day and evening of sightseeing in Seattle, but the group to whom Mr. Beatty, the cruise director, had assigned me was returning to California because one of them had become ill. So they sat gloomily waiting for her to get well enough to make the trip home. In the meanwhile I took a short guided tour and then returned to the hotel room for the rest of the day. That evening I went to the ship just as soon as passengers could go aboard and to my surprise discovered that all the other passengers were still ashore. As the hours passed and daylight turned to dark, that which I had feared came to pass: I was standing alone on the deck looking at the scenery with no one to talk to. So I went below, undressed, and climbed into my bunk. It seemed to me that this cruise could not have had a more miserable beginning.

Early the next day there was a happier turn of events when I went up to the dining room for breakfast. There I met Mr. Douglas, head librarian at the University of Oregon, and his wife, who were assigned to the same table as I. They were a friendly couple in their fifties who were eagerly expecting to enjoy this opportunity to see Alaska which was given to them in exchange for Mr. Douglas' services as cruise librarian.

The fourth member at our table was another unattached girl who was as pleased as I was to find someone in need of company. We joined forces and went places together, which took care of our immediate needs, but in a day or two we each found others who were even more congenial. I had renewed my acquaintance with Ethel Fenwick, an attractive teacher from Klamath Falls, whom I had known slightly at Oregon Normal School when she was there to take some courses in order to keep her teaching certificate current. She and her cabinmate, Nell Thomas, who also taught in Klamath Falls, accepted me as one of them, so whenever there was a day of sightseeing we enjoyed it together. On board ship I spent most of my spare time in their stateroom which was a roomy and well-lighted one on "A" deck. So in the long run, it didn't matter that my cabin was a dingy little one next to the hold, because the only time I used it was during sleeping hours and when I went there to dress for dinner or to find my hat and coat before going ashore to see the sights.

I was signed up for courses in American Literature, Geology with Doctor Packard, and one in Feature Writing taught by Frank Jenkins, the editor of the *Eugene Register-Guard*. Part of my assignment for this class was to keep a diary upon which I would base the travelogue which was the term paper. The first day I wrote this revealing bit of news:

Alongside Vancouver Island—enroute to Alaska.

August 15, 1930

This morning during breakfast at Victoria, B.C., the two customs officials, Canadian and American, sat at our table. They both said they thought they would speak to Mr. Beatty, the cruise director, about the scarcity of men along.

This was something of which the more than one hundred female cruise members were already well aware. A perusal of the passenger list revealed the names of only eight men who were teachers, as were most of the women aboard. Two of the men were youths just out of normal school and the others were middle-aged widowers or bachelors.

Since the cruise director had formerly been Superintendent of Schools for Southeastern Alaska, he had more contacts than the ordinary tour director, making it possible for us to visit interesting Indian settlements usually not seen by tourists. In addition, the ship stopped at all the southeastern Alaska ports including Skagway where we left the ship and went on an all-day train trip over White Pass into the interior of Alaska.

When the S. S. Admiral Rogers arrived at Taku Glacier one rainy morning at five o'clock, the passengers were roused from their warm beds so they could go on deck to watch for huge chunks of ice to drop off the glacier ending at the water's edge. This wouldn't be so remarkable if it happened haphazardly, but often vibrations from the ship's whistle caused the ice to crack and drop off into the water with a mighty splash, so this was what the ship's captain was hoping would happen that morning as he had the whistle blown time after time.

Of course this was interfering with Nature and contrary to everything that today's environmentalists believe in, but the word "ecology" was practically unknown in 1930 so my conscience was clear as I stood there shivering in the cold, waiting for something to happen. But the glacier withstood the vibrations, and those from another ship that had been there just before us trying to do the same thing. When we left the inlet, many of us thought we might just as well have remained in bed.

Grace Brandt in front of totem pole in Nome

Later in the day, we arrived at Juneau, and after returning from a ride out to the Mendenhall Glacier, I walked up town alone looking for the museum. When I found it, which was not hard to do in the small town, it proved to have many interesting exhibits, one of which was the cancelled check from the transaction in which the United States purchased Alaska from Russia. But what I considered even more interesting was the picture of a young woman.

While in the museum I saw the cutest picture of
a girl entitled, "The Wonder Woman of Alaska."
Her name was Mollie (something or other). The
little article under the picture said that she came
out to Alaska all alone from the outside in

1896-1897 to keep a tent roadhouse for the
roughest and most persistent men Alaska ever
knew, but "remained as pure morally as the
driven snow which fell on her roof."

She was an awfully cute-looking girl. I'm so
tired of looking at stuffed birds, ivory carvings,
basketry, etc., in museums that it is a relief to see a
good virtuous girl being featured for a change.

I suppose I took particular notice of Mollie because her story
reinforced what I had been hearing from my mother through the
years. Many a time I had heard "A virtuous woman is always
regarded with respect." And now I saw that one woman had not
only been respected but venerated as a wonder because she had held
out against "persistent" men.

At Sitka I visited the Greek Orthodox church which was am-
bitiously called a cathedral. It was a wooden structure painted
white, and I believe (but am not sure) that the dome was an onion-
shaped one characteristic of Russian churches. The outside was
more impressive than the inside which had varnished wooden floors
and walls covered with white kalsomined paper which sagged
slightly. It was hardly the setting one would expect for the
treasures on display.

These were valuable paintings with exquisitely beautiful
hammered-gold frames, an archbishop's crown encrusted with
pearls and emeralds, and other religious paraphernalia which had
been sent across Siberia and the Bering Sea by a Russian czarina
who had adopted this remote outpost of the Greek Orthodox
Church as her pet charity.

Writing about the church in my diary, I noted that the Russian
Greek Orthodox priest who told us about the history and value of
the church's treasures was a tiny man. He had his set speech and if
one were so imprudent as to ask a question, the whole English
language escaped him and he had to start over again.

There were other aspects to the trip besides sightseeing.

Saturday, August 23, 1930

Nothing much doing except that we are on our
way home and are past Juneau and Petersburg.

Since exams are to be given in three days, the dear
professors are beginning to pour on the long
assignments.

I'm studying geology every possible moment.
Work has at last become a grim reality.

August 26, 1930

Tonight the captain's dinner was enjoyed by all with balloons, horns, rattles, etc., to add to our enthusiasm. The program was made up of two stunts—one by the students—a take-off on the faculty (I was chosen to impersonate the geology professor, Dr. Packard) and the faculty put on a stunt with a totem pole motif—members standing one above the other on chairs, etc. Their explanation of the meaning of the totem was screamingly funny with many "cracks" at the Californians who were so numerous in the enrollment.

We had a dance even if there were fifteen women to one man. Ethel Fenwich and I enjoyed dancing together.‾

The next evening the S. S. Admiral Rogers docked at Seattle where a special train was waiting to take the cruise passengers back to Oregon. The eleven-day cruise complete with room and board plus nine hours of college credit cost $175.00 plus the $35.00 additional amount I spent for souvenirs, tips, and other sundry expenses.

It was one of the never-to-be-forgotten experiences of my lifetime.

WILARK
1930-1931

In September, 1930, when I left home to go to a new teaching position, I was not going into the unknown as had been the case with all my other schools. I had already been in Wilark. Early in the summer, Esther Briggs, my prospective teaching partner, had written to tell me that the house being rented by the district for a teacherage was unfurnished. She offered to meet me at my convenience in St. Helens, twenty miles west of Portland, and take me out to the logging camp so we could learn more about the situation.

One hot day in July I rode the bus to St. Helens where Esther was waiting for me. We drove the short distance to her parents' farm where we ate lunch and then started for Wilark fifteen miles farther on.

On the way there Esther told me that she had been Wilark's lower grade teacher the two previous years but this coming year would be the first time she had ever lived in camp. Before, she had shared the Trenholm school district's teacherage with an older woman who taught there. Esther had gone to her parents' home every weekend and apparently she was planning to do so again.

When we reached the camp, Esther drove directly to the office of Mr. Stendal, the school clerk, because Mr. Stendal was the force behind the school board so he could tell us what we needed to know. He was also the train dispatcher for Clarke Wilson Lumber Company's railroad system and was unusually busy that afternoon. However, he did hand us the keys to both the schoolhouse and the camp house close to the school that he had rented for our use.

We went to look at the schoolhouse which was situated in the lower half of a gently sloping open field. From the outside it appeared to be a big, typical one-room school painted white with a belfry. But after I climbed the steep steps leading to the porch and went inside, I discovered that it had been changed into a two-room school by installing a lengthwise partition down the center. After teaching in Stanfield's well built, spacious, brick high school building, it was a definite let-down, but only a momentary one, for I reminded myself that this district's generous warrants were sure to be cashed on demand. As I surveyed the furnishings and over-all well-kept appearance of the premises, I was sure that the decision to come to Wilark had been a wise one.

From there we went to the nearby camp house where we spent a couple of hours looking around as we tried to decide what must be done to make it habitable. Where would we ever get enough furniture for it? Probably all we could do was to have the essentials—stoves, bed, table and chairs—in place by the time school opened and gradually add more furnishings.

I returned to Portland on the early evening bus and the next day recorded my observations.

Wilark is just a logging camp but, at that, it probably has as many inhabitants as Stanfield. Of course the school there (at Stanfield) was much, much larger because the children came by bus from all directions. However, the Wilark schoolhouse is wonderfully equipped for a country school with carbide lights, a furnace and a janitor to keep it stoked, swings, slides, a large play shed, and very good furnishings inside the building. But I must sadly admit that for all their prosperity, they still have outdoor toilets.

The weather-beaten shack that we are to occupy has never been painted on the outside, just like all the other houses I saw around camp. In the small kitchen there is a sink piped for cold water and the only places for storing things are a few crudely built shelves. The bedroom is about the same size as the kitchen, so there is just enough room for a double bed, dresser, and my wardrobe trunk. No closet, naturally, but a makeshift place to hang clothes has been built in one corner.

The living room is really pretty good-sized (10 x 18) but has only four *small* sliding windows to let in the light.

We're hoping that we'll be able to paper the living room and put some fresh paint on the tongue-and-groove walls in the kitchen and bedroom--but that's something we'll undertake in the distant future. Of course all the tongue-and-groove ceilings are also dingy-looking so we'll have to paint them too, but they're low so that will make it easier.

Although the hills around camp have been cleared of standing timber, I saw quantities of small trees scattered around, which was a shock after the years I've spent in barren eastern Oregon. Our woodshed is set in a grove of trees and there are two more firs by the front porch. Besides that, there is a thicket of saplings growing on the other side of a little creek that flows past the back porch.

On that same day I was also closely observing my future housemate for I knew that when people are paired off by chance, their temperaments are not always compatible. I was hoping that this would not be true of us but I wasn't sure. Esther and I were nearly the same age but she was less experienced because she had always lived close to home except for the time spent at Oregon Normal School in Monmouth. In my diary I described her as a tall, rather prim, blonde girl who wore glasses, and I took note of her abrupt, matter-of-fact manner. I concluded:

As a snap judgment I'd say that Esther isn't a person I'd impulsively choose for a friend, but I probably wouldn't have become friendly with Louise either if we hadn't been forced to live together. Nonetheless we finished that year on the island feeling quite fond of one another. Maybe the same thing will happen again. Anyway, these were first impressions so probably not reliable.

As we exchanged letters after that, I learned that Esther had found surplus furniture in her parents' house which they would loan to us: a bed with bedding, a small gate-leg table and chair set, a dresser, and a sanitary cot that could serve as a sofa. There would be no electricity in our camp house so Esther was also borrowing the kerosene lamps and sadirons (for ironing clothes) that her mother had just recently replaced with electrical appliances.

As she wrote of the many articles she was contributing, I felt almost guilty about her doing so much. Then, when I learned that she and her mother had gone ahead and papered the camp house's living room, I knew for sure that Esther's faults, whatever they might be, did not include laziness or procrastination.

The articles I was contributing tended to be easy to transport and decorative rather than strictly utilitarian. They included scatter rugs, window curtains for every window in the house, as well as cretonne side-drapes for those in the living room, the set of dishes I had used at Summer Lake, two bookcases, including one to be hung on the wall. I also purchased cheerful wallpaper—that which Esther and her mother used to paper the living room—and for the kitchen, red-figured Congoleum floor covering to match the red and white curtains I planned to make.

When I read in a letter that Esther was bringing a sanitary cot, I immediately thought of a way to make it a bright spot in our living quarters. I would cover it with the beautifully-designed and colorful Indian blanket I had bought at the Pendleton Woolen Mills that spring.

When it came to locating a spare stove, we were not so fortunate, so we had to buy an airtight heater ($4.00) and a small cast-iron cookstove ($13.95.) With her father's help, Esther had both in place and ready to be used when school opened.

While all this planning had been in progress, I was spending more than I could afford on clothes and making preparations for the trip to Alaska.

Now the cruise was a thing of the past, and it was September, time to begin teaching again. As I prepared to leave home each fall, I could never decide whether my eagerness to return to the classroom could be attributed to a love for my work or to the prospect of another paycheck. Probably it was a little of both.

On the evening of the second Saturday in September I went to Portland and boarded the bus that was bound for Wilark and Vernonia, a mill town farther on in the Coast Range. The bus followed the Lower Columbia River Highway until it reached St. Helens, where it left the lowlands and headed for the nearby Coast Range

Mountains. While we were still in the foothills, the driver dropped me off at the Briggs' farm where Esther had invited me to spend the night.

Soon after noon on Sunday we set out for Wilark with Mr. Briggs at the wheel. The farther we went, the more logged-off land there was to be seen. Following the road which wound *through* the mountains, *over* the mountains, and *down* the other side, only to climb again, we finally came to a shoestring valley among the hills. This was the site of the logging camp.

Mr. Briggs turned into the first side road we came to. As soon as he left the graveled county road, it didn't take long for me to realize that we were now traveling on a rundown corduroy road made of planks for he began to creep along at a snail's pace. Even then because of the jolting, I had to steady myself by holding onto the car door. Almost immediately, we came to a few camp houses on one side of the road in among young fir trees and beyond them a dense thicket of saplings, on the other side of which was the teacherage with two houses close by facing it across a patch of dry grass.

On the other side of the corduroy road I saw six or seven houses built along two sides of a small, open field. The school grounds were directly behind one of the rows of houses and just a short distance up the road from the teacherage, which explains why Mr. Stendal had chosen that particular house to be the teacherage.

Monday morning, as Esther and I went school, we walked to the end of the corduroy road and after that followed a dirt trail to the schoolhouse. At the proper time I rang the 8:30 bell but it was wasted effort because all the pupils from camp were already there, impatiently waiting for me to unlock the door and let them in. However, the youngsters coming by bus from the Trenholm farming community—also in the Wilark school district—would not be there until later.

When school convened and all the pupils were seated, I saw that every desk in the narrow room was occupied. The desks were arranged in three long rows which were crowded between the five tall windows on one side of the room and a wall of chalkboards on the other. I noticed that there was not much more than just enough room to walk between the rows, placing pupils in much closer contact to each other than they generally are in a classroom. On the other hand, the pupils at the back of the room were much farther away from the teacher's desk—and incidentally, her eagle eye—than is generally the case in a teaching situation.

As was customary, we kept the children just long enough to make a list of their names and tell them what supplies and text books they should bring to school the following morning. As soon as we were alone, my co-worker came into my room to discuss the morning's events. She appeared to be feeling calm and collected. I understood why when we compared our pupil loads. She had sixteen pupils compared to the twenty-four in my room and only three grades while I had four.

Feeling disconcerted, I had counted the number of upper grade children as they came in from the bus that morning. I knew that the uneven distribution of pupils was due to the school board's last minute decision to bus the Trenholm youngsters to Wilark, which had come about after their teacher had resigned late in August because of ill health. Only nine pupils were involved, but six of them were in my room, and those six crowded it to capacity.

However, there was nothing I could do except to try to reconcile myself to existing conditions and suggest that we take an inventory of the supplies on hand in the one small storage closet in each room. After that was done we'd know what we should ask the school clerk to order for the school. When our list was completed, it included not only such essentials as penmanship paper, ink, penpoints, and thumbtacks, but non-essentials including a generous assortment of art materials.

That afternoon as we went to Mr. Stendal's office, I was followng for the first time a route that Esther and I would take several times a week thereafter when we went to the post office to pick up our mail. We left our end of camp and briefly traveled along the graveled county road until we came to a corduroy road which led into the logging camp's headquarters. This road was flanked on one side by a boardwalk and on the other by train tracks built on a railroad bed that had been dug out of the logged-off hillside.

Traveling the boardwalk, we walked past camp houses set wherever the terrain permitted. Sometimes they were built close to the road in long rows, and in other places large groups of houses were set back among groves of fir trees. After following the walk slightly less than a quarter of a mile, we arrived at the heart of the logging camp where the commissary, cookhouse, roundhouse, machine shops, as well as the train dispatcher's office, and health-care center were located. We went into the commissary to notify the postmaster (who was also the storekeeper) that we were in camp and would be receiving mail. While there, we met the bookkeeper who had several children in school, and the one or two other men who had offices in the commissary.

This time we found Mr. Stendal with time on his hands and in a visiting mood. Since I was to be his son's teacher, he called his wife in from their house next door so she could meet me and also renew her friendship with Esther.

We finally settled down to school business. It turned out to be a bewildering experience for me after having lived through the Stanfield school board's desperate efforts to solve their financial problems. When I handed the school clerk the list, I sat back resignedly expecting him to reject most of the non-essentials. Instead he unhesitatingly agreed to send for every single item. Moreover, he urged me to drop in at the J. K. Gill Company (a school supply firm) whenever I was in Portland so I could order and charge to the Wilark school district's account any other school materials we might find useful. In other words, he was handing me a carte blanche to spend as much as my heart desired—no restrictions except that the purchases be for the good of the school. It was simply incredible!

As Esther and I walked back to the teacherage that afternoon, I *did* know that I was teaching in a Clarke Wilson Lumber Company's logging camp. The fact that it was called "Wilark" helped to make this evident. But I had no idea of the company's importance in the lumbering industry. It was not until I had taught there awhile that I began to hear more about it. I learned that it was one of the big lumber companies that had operated around the Great Lakes before moving to the Northwest and that Wilark was the headquarters for all the logging operations that furnished logs for three big Clarke Wilson sawmills located in this area as well as the main mill at Linnton close to Portland. I was amazed when I heard Mr. Stendal describe the extent of the company's network of railroads, one branch of which led to a company town on the Columbia River where ocean-going vessels docked to take on lumber destined for California or the Orient. And later I found it hard to envision Wilark as it must have been when six hundred lunches were prepared daily by the cookhouse employees for the single men's noontime meal in the forests.

Added to them, there would be the camp's family men, so I concluded that there must have been nearly eight hundred in the logging camp's work force during Wilark's heyday. But this was now a thing of the past because by 1930 most of the company's extensive timber holdings had been harvested.

In most ways Wilark was similar to the logging settlements built by other large lumber concerns prior to World War II. However, with regard to its location it was one of the better ones. I realized this was so after I heard my pupils tell of having lived in camps far back in the mountains where the only way in or out was by logging trains. Fortunately, when fate destined me to teach in a logging camp, it led me to one on a bus route and only two hours from a large city.

2

The first time I wrote in my diary after school started, I had no cause for complaint.

September 24, 1930

We've been teaching about two weeks and have already received a paycheck, thanks to the thoughtfulness of our school clerk.

It has been more fun teaching here than I thought it would be. As usual though, any plans I might have had to let things slide just didn't work out. Whenever things "slide," the youngsters become unruly, and I can't stand for that.

According to gossip, the teacher who taught here last year had poor discipline. I must admit that the youngsters certainly had their own sweet method of disposing of time during the first week of school. No attempt was made to do the written assignments, and if one pupil had a book with interesting pictures in it, he was likely to have visitors from up and down the aisle. My good old system of ten problems for every infraction of the rules has been fairly successful in quieting them down. At least I hear rumors of satisfaction among the mothers.

These board members take the prize. Last night when Esther and I attended their meeting, I sat there wondering if it could be only a dream. When I timidly asked if it would be possible to subscribe to two children's magazines, the directors said to the clerk, "Well, George (Mr. Stendal), you'd better get those."

Then all before my bewildered eyes, they—of their own accord—planned to make a movable partition between the two rooms just because I had casually remarked that it must be awfully hard to present a Christmas program in one of the long narrow rooms. All the board members jumped up and rushed to the back of the room where they started to make plans to tear out any and all interfering partitions. The purchase of chalkboards, a new flag pole, jump ropes, more playground equipment, and tables was authorized. Later Esther said that if we'd asked for a sunroom, they would have consented. Of course, the catch is that they are busy men and today may have only vague memories of their spontaneous generosity, like someone after a spree.

However, the minutes of the meeting must have served to remind Mr. Stendal of their promises because he saw to it that they were all fulfilled, including a partition of accordian-type doors, making it possible to have one big room for entertainments.

With this auspicious beginning, I was convinced that few teachers in those depression days were fortunate to have such a teaching position as mine. True, some of the pupils *did* appear to have poor study habits, were strong-willed and uncooperative as yet, but I was sure that I could change all that.

Within a few weeks, it was obvious that the honeymoon with my pupils—if there ever had been one—was over. By then I knew that many of these youngsters were a different breed from those I had faced before. At Midland, the Finnish parents trained their off-spring to be obedient, and in Stanfield most of the pupils were not only cooperative but came from homes where religious training was an important part of their lives. Many Wilark children also showed the results of careful home training, but those who didn't dominated the scene so aggressively that I scarcely noticed the well-behaved pupils.

> I've decided that these youngsters do *not* hail from refined homes. They fight and pull hair and are cheered on by bloodthirsty parents. One girl actually has a fractured rib as a result of the latest encounter. What am I to do with these little heathens who don't understand what it is to act like a lady or gentleman?

The boys and girls were equally violent but I could understand the boys' violence better than I could such behavior in a girl. If a pugnacious girl suspected another girl of writing an uncomplimentary note about her, she followed her adversary out to the playground and attacked her bodily. In my past experience, the one who thought she was wronged would have gone off by herself to weep or else would have come running to me for help, but at Wilark they used a different set of rules.

To make matters worse, the older girls and boys were boy crazy or girl crazy, whichever the case might be. A few of the more knowledgeable ones could find a double meaning in a perfectly innocent remark that one of their classmates or I might make, because they knew all about sex without ever having been in a sex education class.

Since swearing and coarse language were basic elements of their everyday vocabulary, the schoolground rang with profanity. I noted how unimpressed most of my pupils were when I cited Oregon school laws which forbade the use of profane language on the school premises.

Although the course in Adolescent Psychology that I had taken at normal school had been of some help before this time, it did not prepare me for what I was encountering in the logging camp. It took Earl, an eighth grader, to make me aware of one aspect of an adolescent's love life which had not been mentioned in my psychology textbook. He was the product of years spent in logging camps where his mother, a divorcee, had worked as a cookhouse waitress. It's true that Earl had not attained his full height yet, but he was mature in other ways. Already his cheeks were covered with the soft down that precedes a beard, and he had an eye for the girls. But that was nothing to be concerned about until he turned his attention to me.

My chief worry this past week has been Earl, who is the most mature fourteen-year-old boy I've ever known. Lately it has bothered me like the dickens because wherever I am in the classroom, I can feel his adoring gaze. I don't know what has caused this sudden ardor, but the fact remains that it is there—and I don't know what to do about it.

It's hard to convince the rest of my pupils that I'm a figure of authority while one of their classmates is looking at me with great longing in his eyes. It's even worse when Earl blithely "kids" me with a worldly-wise line that he's probably picked up by listening to his mother's boyfriends.

Since Earl lived close by, Esther and I hired him to chop wood for us. During that period of time when I was the center of his attention, he dropped in for a visit as soon as he had split and carried the wood to the back porch. Then as I hurried around, working at my household chores, he sat in silence intently watching my every move. In silence, because having only Esther and me to hear him, he was less inclined to display his worldly-wise line.

Another memory in connection with Earl concerns the time that he was staying in after school to finish his written work. A salesman who had previously sold me an insurance policy came by that evening to work out the final details. Instead of being required to go to a doctor for a physical examination, I was allowed to fill out a questionnaire with the usual information: my height, weight, chest measurement, etc. When I was unable to give my chest measurement, the young salesman handed me a five-foot tape measure.

I was wearing a dress made of soft silk that day, and as I pulled the tape tightly across my bust, I could feel Earl's intense interest. I became so flustered when I saw both the boy and the salesman watching me that I started measuring from the wrong end of the tape. As I fumbled with it and hurriedly read the number, I was startled to hear myself announcing that I had a fifty-seven inch bust!

Earl was of a fickle nature so he soon turned his attention to one of the eighth grade girls who squealed with delight when he chased her around the school ground. That must have brought Earl far more satisfaction than having a crush on an unresponsive teacher.

Through the pages of my diary I worried about the children's pugnacity but seldom mentioned names or gave details of a particular fracas because fights were so commonplace. However, I did write in detail about one other challenge because it was a crisis in my teaching experience at Wilark.

The trouble started when Dominick tripped another boy who was walking down the aisle during schooltime. I saw the incident and immediately assigned Dominick ten problems to be worked during recess as a punishment. But when it was time for a break, he stood up and filed out of the room with the others despite my protests. During recess I decided to send him home because I was sure that his father, who had a responsible position in camp, would back me up.

Fifteen minutes later I rang the bell for the youngsters to come in. When Dominick appeared, I stood in the doorway and told him that he'd have to go home. The boy was a muscular, 140-pound eighth grader who was heavier and stronger than I, so he brushed me aside and went on in.

In all my other schools, I had insisted upon being treated respectfully, and I intended to continue demanding respect. Also, I could feel the rest of the pupils watching for my next move. As soon as Dominick was seated, I went to his desk and began to shake him and continued until he had tears in his eyes and I, too, was almost sobbing. Then I walked to the front and began to speak to the roomful of subdued youngsters. I told them that I had been hired to teach the school and that it was impossible to do so unless I was the person in charge. Then I went on to explain that I would be cheating them and the school district if I did not maintain a quiet, orderly classroom in which they could learn. As I finished and looked around, I sensed that the children were receptive to my point of view. Also they now knew that I would resort to physical punishment if I had to, which was all that some of them understood. But I was not feeling triumphant as I wrote in my diary that night about the day's happenings.

I hate to use force to make youngsters behave.
In the end Dominick did the problems which he
had said he would *never* do, but he did not change
his mind because I shook and forcefully punished
him. He gave in after he heard me tell them all
why I had to insist upon obedience.

Even yet, I'm not sure that there was any other way that I could
have brought about Dominick's compliance that day.

This one time that I punished a camp child physically may have
had an effect upon the behavior of pupils who enrolled at Wilark
many months later. During the following year a sixth grade boy
entered school and he proved to be disobedient and resentful of my
disciplinary measures. While he and some of the other boys were
eating their lunch one day, I overheard him telling them what he intended to do to me. One of his listeners responded in an undertone,
but I heard the word, "Dominick" although Dominick was then in
high school. After that I was fairly sure that those who had been in
school when I went there to teach passed the story of Dominick on
to newcomers, and thus saved me the bother of dealing with a
similar incident all over again.

As could be expected, I was discovering that some of the parents
were as difficult as their offspring. This became evident just after
the first monthly tests.

When I went to the commissary today, I found
that the Traveling Library we had ordered from
Salem (the State Library) had arrived. We are going to keep the Traveling Library at the teacherage
so adults can come evenings and weekends to borrow books. We were in a flurry of unpacking the
books and deciding where to put them when there
was a knock at our door. It was a girl with a note
from her mother who wanted to know why the
bearer of the note and her sister had failed to pass
the geography test.

I was tired anyway, in fact exhausted, from
teaching all day but somehow had become involved with the library books anyway. On top of
everything else, to have this complaining note arrive was just too much. I gently pushed Ruth
toward the door and said, "We'll talk about that
tomorrow, Ruth."

75

Wilark school pupils and teachers, 1931-1932. Top row, left to right: Harry Bryson, Miss Brandt, Ruth Makinster, Clifford Hartung, Elaine Makinster, Lillian Wittnebel, Aletha Kromrey, ? ?, ? Hartung, Angelina Serafin, Miss Briggs. Row two from top: ? ?, Donita Bryson, John Wilverding, Virgil Hewett, ? ?, ?, ? ?, Ruth Wittnebel. Rows 3 and 4 and part of bottom row are made up of primary youngsters with whom the author had little contact, so cannot name them. Bottom row: ? ?, ? ?, ? ?, Benny Brown [with ball], ? Bryson, ? ?, Erland Hill.

I thought that would be just the beginning, but
the dear mama didn't appear as I had anticipated.
She's written several hostile notes, but Esther says
she always does that just to try teachers out. The
joys of teaching!

Another time two mothers joined forces and came to school to
express their opinion of my teaching ability.

> December 8, 1930
> Today I had the first experience of my teaching
> career with a *really* irate parent. I can't get one of
> my eighth grade boys to work—maybe it is my
> fault—but more likely it is because he has been
> passed on from grade to grade whether he was
> ready for the next one or not. Now he's in the
> eighth grade and can't read any of the books for
> that grade or do the simplest arithmetic. Anyway,
> he's sixteen years old and hasn't a chance in a
> thousand of passing the eighth grade exams. He's
> pretty awful slow, besides not wanting to try, so I
> thought we'd have a talk (his mother and I) to see
> if that might not help.
> She came rushing into the schoolroom after
> school all worked up, saying that I had pets, that I
> was cranky, and that I certainly wasn't equal to
> the last teacher. She ended up by saying that I'd
> better get her boy through the eighth grade or
> she'd "see." Oh, glory! What's the use?

The woman's husband was the local moonshiner, so she had for-
tified herself for the meeting by sampling some of his liquor. Ac-
companying her was one of her friends who also reeked of bootleg
whiskey.

When the first woman stopped to catch her breath, her friend
took over and aired her grievances. They were many, and all of
them concerned her son, one of my pupils who was totally unprepared to do seventh grade work. He, too, was lazy and spent far
more time thinking of how to get out of work than in studying. I
used to be astonished at how many ways he could cheat. That
afternoon the seventh grader's mother berated me on and on
because her boy failed in the tests every month and his report card

reflected this fact. As she was leaving, she flung out one last insult, "Since my kid isn't learning anything here, I'm going to move to Camp 8 (another Clarke Wilson logging camp) where he will have a *good* teacher for a change."

Mrs. Howard, the janitor, was cleaning up after school so she overheard the women's tirades and hurried to tell her neighbor, Mrs. Hewett, about the noisy parent-teacher conference. Mrs. Hewett, a newly appointed member of the school board who lived nearby, came to the teacherage as soon as she saw I was home. First, she told me "not to feel bad" about the women's abuse because everyone in camp knew they were unreasonable and quarrelsome. Then she assured me that the board members were more than satisfied with the way I was conducting school. And since Mrs. Hewett had a well-behaved daughter who did not find it difficult to make high grades in the monthly tests, she went on to give me her personal vote of confidence, all of which helped to restore confidence to my bruised and battered ego.

3

During the previous summer Esther and I had written back and forth enthusiastically planning to make the teacherage attractive and homelike. However, after we moved in, we made few improvements—even though we had the materials on hand to do so—because we were busy with school work during the week and went away every weekend. The only good features the place had were the freshly-papered walls in the living room and colorful curtains at the windows. These scarcely compensated for the worn and dirty woodwork throughout the house or the lack of furniture in the living room (one stove, two bookcases, a cot covered with my Indian blanket, and two straight-back chairs).

One October weekend when I remained in camp, I became so restless that I started to paint the gate-leg table Esther had brought from home. A week later, after I'd applied three coats of yellow paint to the table and chair set, I started in on the dingy woodwork and Esther also became interested.

For a week or so we hurried home after school to paint and I continued to work weekends, so we ended up with the walls, ceilings, and bare floors in the living room and bedroom looking fresh and clean. There was a Congoleum rug on the kitchen floor. In one last burst of enthusiasm we put colorful paper on the cupboard shelves and red-checked curtains (to match those at the windows) in front of the opening under the sink.

Although it was hard work, I enjoyed the project because it was a relaxing change from teaching and I was proud of the results. But we hadn't found a way to add furniture to the living room without spending money.

The problem took care of itself. We heard that there were odds and ends of furniture belonging to the Wilark School District in the Trenholm teacherage. When the truck carrying the furniture arrived at our place, the driver and his helper unloaded a Congoleum rug for the living room, a crude kitchen table with two chairs, a huge, uncomfortable-looking homemade rocker, and the upright piano that had been in the Trenholm schoolhouse. Now that we had the extra table, we moved the gate-leg table and chairs out of the kitchen into the living room, in the corner near the stove. I was quite pleased.

> Except for that monstrosity of a homemade rocker, the room looks cozy to my way of thinking. We're hoping to replace it with a small Windsor rocker and then the room will look quite all right.

Esther and I both liked to be systematic and orderly. We arose at 6 a.m., which may have been an indication of Esther's having lived on a farm all her life, but perhaps it wasn't Esther's background so much as the example set by the loggers each morning hurrying to catch the train that took them out to the logging operation.

> This morning I managed to sleep through the usual 4:40 a.m. whistle, but at 5:40 a logging train broke the daily routine by whistling shrilly at every tie it crossed. When another train left at 6:00, it was just too much. Esther and I had a general consultation with both flashlight, watches, and the alarm clock brought into play. When a logger started running up the planked road outside our

79

window, we thought nothing less than a fire in the machine shops could be taking place. I never did find out what it was all about, but I do know we lost an hour's sleep.

There was plenty of time so we cooked and ate a hearty breakfast every morning and then made the teacherage neat and clean before leaving for school at eight o'clock. We took turns rushing home at noon to build a fire in the cookstove so we could heat left-overs or a can of soup for lunch. In the meantime, one of us remained at school to supervise, and at 12:30 we exchanged places. Under this arrangement we each were away from the schoolroom only thirty minutes, but how restful it seemed to be alone in the quiet cabin for even that brief interval!

Thanks to our airtight heater, the living room was never cold when we entered it at noon, because we stoked the stove with big chunks of thick bark before we went away in the morning. By almost closing the damper in the stovepipe, we caused the fire to smolder slowly and not burn out before our return.

Although I was inclined to be methodical by temperament, Esther was even more so and made the suggestion that we have a duty schedule to follow. From then on we not only knew what was to be done each day but whose turn it was to do it. We took turns preparing the evening meal—Monday, Esther; Tuesday, Grace, etc., with the one not cooking responsible for washing dishes and cleaning the kitchen after dinner.

The daylight hours in our end of the logging camp were fewer than elsewhere because we lived in a hollow among the hills where the sun set early in the wintertime. Besides that, our house had small windows and was shaded by fir trees. As we had to light the kerosene lamps at four o'clock on gloomy days, keeping them in order was important. One evening during the week, whether they needed it or not, it was the chore of one of us to wash the lamp chimneys in hot sudsy water and trim the wick. Whoever was keeper of the light that week also kept the lamps filled with coal oil.

Again these were Esther's ideas, not mine. Always before in my experience with kerosene lamps, I had not paid attention to them except when they needed oil, or soot was visible on the chimney. As for the wicks, I had never trimmed them until the flame began to flicker because of built-up carbon. I became a convert to Esther's good housekeeping practices, though, when I saw the always-shiny chimneys and realized that we never had to interrupt some other activity to give emergency treatment to an ailing lamp.

The after-school hours on Thursday were set aside for changing bed linen and cleaning the house from top to bottom. If I were to be gone over the weekend, I heated water after we finished the evening meal so I could do my washing, including the one sheet and one pillow slip that were my share to launder. Esther took her laundry home every Friday so the other sheet and pillow slip would be attended to there. Then I shampooed my hair and finally, just before I retired, took a bath in the washtub.

When I spoke of our detailed work schedule to one of my friends in camp, she thought we were going to ridiculous extremes. To her way of thinking, it was more friendly to share the work spontaneously, but for us a schedule was successful because neither of us objected to a rigid division of chores, and each of us did her part. I must confess, however, that I sometimes wished that Esther wouldn't always work so hard. Then I could have relaxed occasionally instead of constantly feeling obliged to do my part.

Wilark teachers Esther Briggs and Grace Brandt posing on the school playground.

After dinner we either read library books, did school work, or listened to the secondhand battery-powered console radio that Esther had bought for our enjoyment. The radio filled our leisure hours with interest and gave us a wonderful sense of being in immediate contact with large urban centers and the world of entertainment. We eagerly listened to the "Lucky Strike Hit Parade" to learn which songs had been most popular that week. Like almost all radio listeners, we were absorbed in the experiences of Amos 'n Andy and were Rudy Vallee fans. If I stayed in camp over the weekend, I tuned in on the "One Man's Family" radio series Sunday night and learned of the latest happenings in the Barber family. Before we retired at 10:30 p.m., we switched to the news to see if anything startling had happened since 6:00 when we had listened before.

It was also during the evenings that we were reminded of the heating problems in our low-ceilinged living room. If the chunk of wood we threw into the heater had pitch in it, as it did so often, the sides of the stove became red-hot in no time. Anyone sitting close by began to roast. This applied to both of us because the corner close to the stove was the only available spot for the table that held the kerosene lamp. After standing up to move my chair away from the heat, I wrote this comment when I was seated again on the *far* side of the table:

> Whew! It's hot in here. As usual, this room has an average temperature of 98.6°. Over on the couch under the window it must be a chilly fifty degrees and here at the table by the stove, ninety-five degrees. And my conservative estimate is that any place near the ceiling is 145°. Average it up: 98.6° or thereabouts.

4

Since Wilark was only a two-hour bus ride away from Portland, my weekends presented a variety of interesting possibilities which helped me forget the problems at school. Usually I rode the Friday evening bus to Portland where I spent the night with Louise Sullivan who had been my fellow teacher at Midland. Now she was working as a stenographer in the city and lived in a rooming house which was convenient for me to go to because it was only five blocks from the Greyhound Bus Depot. We went out for all of our meals since there were no cooking facilities in Louise's room, and this made me feel less concerned that I might be imposing on my friend's hospitality.

If there were good movies or a road-show in town, I stayed with Louise until it was time to return to Wilark Sunday evening. But more often I spent Saturday forenoon shopping and then rode the Mt. Scott streetcar to Lents Junction (the end of the car line), where my father was always patiently waiting with the Model T, no matter how far behind schedule I was.

Other times I was guest of one or the other of my married girl friends whom I had known since childhood. One of these was Mable Tacheron whom I had visited when she and her husband, Frank, lived in Pendleton and I was teaching in Stanfield. Now their home was in Portland again, so one Saturday after I had ridden to the city with my camp neighbor, Mrs. Hewett, I went to visit the Tacherons. Upon my arrival, Mable told me that there was going to be a party at their house that night, which sounded like fun, because it would give me a chance to be with friends whom I had not seen for a long time.

I reached Mable's house about noon and that evening Ruth, Julie, and Dorothy and their husbands came over for a waffle feed. Later three more couples whom I'd never met before joined us. We danced and I had a busy evening being rushed by the husbands who were imbibing a bit too much homemade beer. Around 1 a.m. all of the men contributed money for the cause and they sent out for Chinese noodles.

83

There was only one unattached man in the crowd. He was all right, I guess—tall, a good dancer, and had a nice singing voice. He was rather interested in me, I think, but I saw no evident desire to lay his life and fortune at my feet. Anyway, he's a salesman working out of Pendleton, so it's not likely that I will ever see him again. It was an interesting and lively evening—something to do.

I was surprised to see the men drinking beer at the party because I had known several of them ever since high school days and this was the first time I had ever seen them drink anything stronger than soda pop or root beer. From experience, I knew that loggers, cowboys, and Finnish fishermen did not let a mere Prohibition Amendment discourage their consumption of liquor, and according to the news media another segment of the population patronized speakeasies and carried liquor-filled pocketflasks. But in my experience previous to this time, the run-of-the-mill citizens, those like my friends, had abided by the law and had not considered an alcoholic beverage an absolute necessity in order to have a successful party. However, the girls at Mable's party let their husbands do the drinking for the family, so I suppose they still thought it wasn't proper for a woman to drink alcoholic beverages.

Later on, when I spent a weekend with my friends, Sylvia and Leib Riggs in Clatskanie, I discovered that they, too, had changed their drinking habits. Three years before when I had been teaching in Midland, they were teetotalers but now they gleefully showed me a stock of homemade beer, and at their party that night they served cocktails to both men and women. I couldn't help but be surprised by this changed attitude toward the use of alcohol in my formerly law-abiding friends.

I recalled that five years ago in Summer Lake I had been afraid to go to a dance with a man who might drink while we were there because I knew that I would be gossiped about and suspected of being fast, even though I, myself, hadn't tasted a single drop of the home-brew.

My Christmas vacation in 1930 was an unusually interesting one because part of the time had been spent in Klamath Falls visiting Ethel Fenwick whom I had met on the Alaskan cruise.

When I arrived back in camp after my vacation, I was of two

minds. I was happily thinking of the parties and dances I had attended in Klamath Falls and at the same time realizing that the morrow would bring me face to face with the same obstreperous youngsters who had been there before Christmas.

The truth was that I dreaded the days ahead. So I decided that the time had come to have an understanding with Esther about our unequal class loads which had been an unspoken bone of contention between us all year. Esther's contract explicity stated that the primary teacher should teach the fifth grade if the upper grade enrollment was noticeably larger, but the school board hadn't stepped in to make an adjustment. And Esther hadn't offered to change the status quo even though she had only fourteen pupils in three grades by Christmas while I had twenty-six pupils in grades 5, 6, 7, and 8. So there was no doubt in my mind but what my co-worker should be teaching the fifth grade. And it had not helped matters when she intimated that if she were their teacher, she'd not tolerate some of the upper graders' behavior.

We had never brought the subject of the uneven class loads out into the open, so it smoldered beneath the surface of our relationship making any real friendship impossible, although we performed our household chores in apparent harmony.

The matter was settled when I asked her to take part of my work load and she somewhat reluctantly complied with my request. With this source of dissension out of the way, we gradually became friendly companions instead of being two individuals who conscientiously shared the housework.

It was a joy to discover a few weeks later that I was actually liking my work. I was more relaxed and for the first time that year loyally thought of those under my care as being "my" pupils. One afternoon, even though I was tired, I decided to tell of the changes that had taken place.

> To be fair to Wilark, I must write while I'm feeling at peace with the world. This past week or so the children—every last one of them—have been cooperative and friendly. They are buckling down to work, so it almost seems like the old days when I was teaching at Midland and Stanfield.
>
> Evidently all it took to bring about this long-

desired harmony was a little understanding on my
part. Now I find myself looking upon everyone in
the room as interesting and a distinct personality
(even those who get into trouble) instead of thinking of the whole lot of them as rough, tough,
camp-kids. Of course they aren't perfect by any
means, so there are fights on the schoolground
every once in a while, but while we are inside, we
are quite civilized.

There were several reasons why I had such a different outlook.
In the first place I returned to camp refreshed from a change of
scenery during the holidays. More important was the fact that I
had a lighter teaching load and consequently stopped being resentful.

But probably most important was the change in my attitude
toward teaching as a whole after I read a pamphlet that came in the
mail one day in January. The pamphlet was entitled "State Course
of Study for Moral Education." I can remember exactly where I
was sitting and the intense interest, almost excitement, I felt as I
perused its contents. Never before had I read an Oregon State
Department of Education publication that denounced one of the
accepted school practices as this one did.

*"Corporal punishment is degrading to both the child and
teacher."*

I continued to read and came to another startling break with the
traditional philosophy of strict control in the classroom.

"Absolute quiet is not necessary if the noise is that of a busy
room."

What a change this was from the long-standing demand for a
schoolroom "quiet enough to hear a pin drop!" Somehow, this
assurance that absolute quiet was not always desirable freed me of
the burden of striving for perfect order in that long, crowded
schoolroom. From then on, I put most of my efforts into being a
good teacher, not a strong disciplinarian.

5

In September, as soon as Erma Christensen heard that a Miss Brandt was teaching in Wilark, she came to find out if I were Johnny Brandt's sister. Her maiden name had been Erma McTaggart and that was the name I remembered her by when she said that she and my older brother at one time had belonged to the same group of friends. When she saw that I was indeed Johnny's sister, she treated me like a long-lost friend. Both of us had attended Gilbert Elementary School on the outskirts of Portland but Erma had been an upper grader when I was in the first grade.

We knew some of the same people in our old neighborhood and she had taught school before her marriage, so we were off to a good start. When I met her husband, Mike, he also heartily made me feel like one of their family.

During the autumn Erma with her four-year-old Bobby in tow often strolled over to see me at the schoolhouse late in the afternoon or came to the teacherage on Saturday to get a book from the Traveling Library. Then she stayed for a visit.

On the days that it was Esther's turn to cook dinner, I went to the commissary to pick up our mail and as I passed Erma's house on the way home, I'd drop in for a brief chat. Also during the weekends if I felt restless or lonely, it was good to know that a warm welcome awaited me at the Christensens.

Saturday afternoon I'd finished making out report cards and didn't feel in the mood to read a book, so I went over to the Christensens, taking along some silk stockings that needed to be darned on the heels. I'd fully intended to leave as soon as I'd finished my darning, but when Erma invited me to stay to dinner, I couldn't resist.

I couldn't resist because I knew that Erma was a superb cook in spite of having only a small cast-iron cookstove to work with. Still, the stove was in keeping with the rest of the kitchen furnishings which were comprised of a cheap, but sturdy, drop-leaf table and four chairs, Bobby's high chair, a set of dishes, silverware, plus a good assortment of cooking utensils.

That day when Erma took me into the living room, she insisted upon my sitting in the comfortable rocker and she went into the kitchen to find a straight-backed chair for herself. The only other piece of living room furniture was the wood-burning heater. The bedroom held a double bed and Bobby's crib. That was all, except for the clothes hanging on nails pounded into one wall and a couple of suitcases.

Their home's barren appearance could not be blamed on a lack of money. Ever since Mike had left home to go to the logging camps at the age of sixteen, he had received top pay—up to ten dollars a day—when the average bluecollar worker was being paid four dollars or less. Mike, like most loggers, wanted to be free to quit his job and move on to another camp whenever he felt the impulse, so he limited their household possessions to what could be carried in the back seat of his car and a small trailer.

Erma kept the rooms neat and clean and tried to make their home more attractive by hanging curtains at the tall, narrow windows, but it would take more than curtains to achieve that goal. However, it was a shelter from the elements and probably looked quite inviting to Mike in the winter when he entered its warmth after a day's work, followed by a long ride on the unheated logging train. Certainly the barrenness didn't have an adverse effect on my good times when I was there. Whether the walls were painted or unpainted, the rooms furnished or unfurnished struck me as being unimportant.

However, I could not help comparing their house with the others I'd had an opportunity to see when Esther and I solicited contributions for the American Red Cross during a fund-raising drive that fall. As I sat there darning, I looked around and came to the conclusion that this camp house probably was one of the most simply furnished ones I'd seen. Some men in camp did not suffer from the typical logger's restless urge to move, and in that case time and effort were put into improving a family's dwelling. At times people even went to extremes.

I thought of one of the houses in our end of the logging camp. Its living room—the only room Esther and I saw when we were there selling Red Cross buttons—had painted woodwork, figured paper on the walls, a Congoleum rug, stiffly starched lace curtains, two rocking chairs, and a big, nickel-trimmed heater as well as a wide daybed covered with a white ruffled spread and half a dozen plump sofa pillows. Bric-a-brac, including plumed Kewpie dolls, were placed in every possible nook and surface around the room. The master of this household, a middle-aged mechanic, had worked at Wilark for years, and from the appearance of the over-decorated living room, the thought of moving had never entered his wife's mind.

When Mike returned from work that Saturday while I was there with my darning, he paused at the back door to remove his calked boots which would have dug pits in the floors if worn inside. After that he used several basins full of soapy warm water to scrub away the worst of the grime from his hands and face. This was not a once-over-lightly process, for during the day his face and hands, as well as his outer clothing, had acquired a layer of bark dust, dirt, and pitch mixed together.

As Mike waited somewhat impatiently for the rest of us to join him at the table, he appeared to be ravenously hungry, even though he had eaten a huge breakfast at 5:30 a.m. and undoubtedly had devoured all the food in his well-filled lunch pail. As soon as we sat down, he commenced to fill his plate with roast beef, potatoes, gravy, cooked vegetables, bread and butter, and peach preserves. After he had stowed away his fill of these, plus generous cups of coffee, he topped them off with a big wedge of butterscotch pie swathed in whipped cream. Despite regularly partaking of such meals, he continue to have the lean, wiry build characteristic of a logger while poor Erma, who also ate them, was mourning the loss of her slender figure.

The loggers and their wives had to be up and about at such unbelievable hours on work days that they went to bed early, but they still had to have something interesting to do in those hours between supper time and bedtime. This was a problem if one didn't like to read, or own a radio, as was true of Mike. But he *did* have a pleasing baritone voice and enjoyed singing with the piano so he was always willing to come to our place whenever Erma passed on the information that Esther had bought some new sheet music.

In addition to enthusiastically blending my voice with the others, I generally contributed to the occasion by passing around the fudge I'd made earlier. All too often it had turned out to be the kind that had to be eaten with a spoon, but our long-suffering guests politely ate it and were willing to come again.

One of the Christensens' favorite stories concerned their first date. At that time Erma was teaching the first grade in the Lynch district near Portland and Mike was a logger in the Coast Range Mountains. One Saturday he went to the big city in search of a good time and, quite by chance, ended up at a dance in Erma's neighborhood. He found her attractive and before the evening ended asked her for a date. She agreed. However, he failed to write down her address or telephone number so two weeks later when he went to pick her up with a taxi (since he did not own a car) he spent fifteen dollars—a lot of money in those days—for cab fare before he finally located her home. This was the significant part of the story. Mike's reckless disregard for money flattered Erma and convinced her that he was sincerely interested so she took him seriously.

Now as a housewife in a logging camp, she seemed happy, in spite of sometimes being bored, and was still very much in love with her tall good-looking young husband. They both were devoted to their four-year-old son and were systematically putting money aside for his college education.

By mutual agreement the family's finances were handled by Erma who was the better manager of the two. They hoped to end up with something to show for a lifetime of hard work, which was not the case in many logger's experience. With this end in view, the Christensens were buying land in the suburbs of Portland on the installment plan, paying for a twenty-year endowment policy, and had invested in oil-well stock. They could afford to make all the payments because the cost of living at Wilark was extremely low. Rent for the company owned houses was ten dollars per month with water and firewood provided free of charge. The only other expenses were the food bill (theirs must have been considerable), kerosene to provide light, and gasoline for their car. Unfortunately, the success of their plans to save for the future was contingent upon a steady income at the present level, and during the Depression things didn't always work out that way.

I first met Mary Troy when she brought me the attendance records from the Trenholm School where she had taught for a few days until the board decided to transport the pupils to Wilark.

A young woman who taught the Trenholm

youngsters for a while came by today. As we .
visited, I learned that she taught in various places,
including some places in eastern Oregon that were
as bad as Summer Lake. She's married to the man
who runs the commissary and is camp postmaster.
He must have an extremely good-paying job—
or else there is a rich uncle in the background—
because Mrs. Troy told me that they vacationed
this summer at Baniff and Lake Louise (all to the
tune of $16 per day at the hotels.) Now they
are busily planning a trip to Europe for next
summer.

I see that there are cliques here in camp, just as
there are in most communities, and I've decided
that the Troys must be members of the elite group.
After I knew more about the Troys, I realized that, although
Jimmy Troy did earn a good salary, it was their stringent economy
beforehand that made their travels possible.

**Mary Troy standing beside her front porch,
wearing the elaborately embroidered daytime
pajamas she made for herself.**

The friendship between Mary Troy and me did not develop rapidly because we lived at the opposite ends of camp. Troys' house was in a little meadow located along the road to Vernonia, instead of being on the way which led into the commissary. Calling on her meant making a special trip in her direction, and of course it was just as far for her to come to me. However, she went out of her way to offer me a ride to Portland soon after we met and the following week I walked over to her place.

October 26, 1930

I went to see Mrs. Troy for the first time one nice evening last week when it was not my turn to cook. Her house is charming and spacious-looking—in spite of the fact that it has only three rooms—because her interior decorating was a planned project and shows exquisite taste. Compared to her house, this teacherage with its motley assortment of furnishings looks pretty tawdry. Still, I must loyally point out that, even so, ours is better than most of the homes in Wilark.

I do believe that Mrs. Troy and I could be close friends if we'd see each other often, but we live so far apart that it is hard to become better acquainted.

I had heard about the head engineer's house which was a converted boxcar so tastefully furnished by his English wife that it was a work of art, but of all the houses I actually saw in Wilark that of Jimmy and Mary Troy was in a class by itself. They had painted the walls and open ceilings in all three rooms a neutral buff color which made a pleasing background for their fine furniture. Ruffled white curtains covered the tall double windows in the living room and a teacart with a coffee service stood in front of the windows. What impressed me the most throughout the house were the new floors which had been varnished, covered with a protective coat of wax, and polished to a high gloss. Mary's hand-crocheted scatter rugs, which she had made to blend with the color of the walls, added to the living room's charm. Since their camp house was built on skids so it could be picked up and loaded onto a flatcar, they unhesitatingly made improvements without fear of being forced to leave their house behind if the company moved them to a different location.

As time passed, we became increasingly friendly.

December 15, 1930
The Troys took me into town last Saturday.

January 26, 1931
Mary Troy said that she might go to Portland again this coming Saturday, and if she does, I may go with her. I must bestir myself and get my washing done tonight because Mary has asked me over for dinner tomorrow evening. I wish she lived closer so I could run in often for a good chat with her. She's an understanding soul and has mastered the art of keeping the conversation in the other person's territory. It's a gift to not talk too much about one's self.

January 29, 1931
I enjoyed myself over at Mary's last Friday. She had the table carefully set with her good Spode china and we ate by candlelight which made it seem like a real dinner party. I was sorry that I had only bothered to change to a fresh school dress.

The next morning Mary came by early and we went to Portland in their impressive Buick car which is positively a picture of luxury.

In Portland we shopped around a bit looking for a dress for Mary, but instead we found one in a small black print that is my type. Although it cost fourteen dollars and my conscience therefore told me to forget the dress, Mary persuaded me to buy it. Now I'm glad that I did, because it is so becoming with its peplum and softly draped mid-calf length skirt.

February 6, 1931
Last weekend was quite a bit of fun. Both Mary Troy and Erma Christensen came over Saturday afternoon. The stupid cliquishness of this place! Mary and Erma don't visit each other because Erma is considered to be lower on the camp's social scale just because Mike is a logger while Mary's husband is a white-collar worker. But the three of us had a good time anyway. We had a good old talk and found solutions to all the world's problems.

April 6, 1931

Tuesday after school I went to see Mary, but it was late when I got there so she wanted me to come back the next afternoon. I half agreed, but when I arrived here at the house, I decided that I couldn't because Esther already had cooked two nights in a row. So the next day I hurried to Mary's to tell her that I would not be able to stay for a visit. As we chatted briefly, she mentioned that she'd heard that bus fares to Portland were going up to $2.50. I was all excited and perturbed by the news.

Not long after I'd arrived back home, Mary came rushing in to tell me that she'd checked her information about the fares and learned that she had been wrong. We laughed and decided that we were showing true concern for one another by my running to tell her not to expect me, and her making the mile trip (there and back) to tell me she had been mistaken about the raise in bus fares.

I hardly ever met Mary's husband except when I went for the mail. He put in long hours at the commissary, opening it up at 5:45 a.m. so the loggers could shop before work, and he kept it open until 6 p.m. every day except Sunday.

Quite often, however, I had dinner with them on Friday if I stayed in Wilark, and then Jimmy and I had a chance to become acquainted. He, too, had a good singing voice, so Esther and I invited the Troys over for an evening of singing. However, his strong baritone voice reverberated in our low-ceilinged living room so powerfully and so completely drowned out the rest of us that we might just as well have remained silent. Even Jimmy recognized that his voice was not suited to our small room, so we spent the rest of that evening talking and eating the ubiquitous plate of fudge. After than when they came over, it was in response to our invitation to have dinner or to come just for a visit.

These two couples, The Christensens and the Troys, were the only people with whom I became well acquainted while I was in

Wilark. However, others among the white-collar workers made overtures. Once, Mr. Bryson, the bookkeeper, and his wife invited Esther and me to dinner, and another time we were invited to the Brown home. Mr. Brown was a trained male nurse who took care of the industrial health services in camp. Also generous-hearted Mr. Stendal and his family came by one Sunday to take me to Portland for an expensive dinner and a show. All these were friendly gestures which I appreciated even if they didn't lead to deeper friendships.

6

One did not need to be an unusually discerning person to see that Mary Troy was a happily married woman. She had been in her mid-twenties and Jimmy past thirty when she went to teach in a logging camp where he was the bookkeeper. Mary told me how relieved they were when they learned after a few dates that they were both Catholics. Mary was a Titian-blond Italian and Jimmy a black-haired Irishman. Without a religious barrier in their way, they were free to let themselves fall in love. Since they were both so complete-ly happy after having spent several years looking for just the "right one," Mary was convinced that their meeting was a God-ordained miracle. Now that everything had turned out so well for her, she felt sorry for her unmarried friends, including me. She still believed in miracles but thought she might do her bit in my behalf just in case I did not rate divine intervention.

While I was over at Mary's the other day, she told me that she and Jimmy have been trying to think of a beau for me. They've gone through the list of single men in camp but can't find anyone that they deem suitable.

I looked over all the men in the bunkhouses that time when Esther and I sold Red Cross buttons, and I must say that I agree with her. Also, I've been somewhat wary of loggers ever since one of them tore the bus door off its hinges while coming back from a weekend on Portland's Skid Road. Sometimes the loggers are drunk and pretty wild when they get on the bus to come back to camp. Makes me glad I'm sitting on the other side of a glass partition with the bus driver.

Then Mike decided to play Cupid.

February 5, 1931

Tuesday evening I made candy because Esther and I had told the Christensens that we would expect them at our place that night. Over the weekend Esther had bought the sheet music to some of the latest song hits, so we knew that they would want to try them out.

Imagine our surprise when a tall, good-looking redhead came in with them! It was the famous Charlie, a locomotive engineer about whom Mike has teased me so much. Mike, having a matchmaker's instinct, has enjoyed talking a lot to us about each other. Often he concludes his praises of his friend by summing them all up into one sentence, "Charlie's a hell of a good guy!"

So there you are!

The funny part is that Charlie had seen me on the bus and watched me talking to the bus driver all the way from Portland one Sunday night. As soon as we were introduced, he said he thought that he'd seen me before and then launched into a humorous account of how he'd had the door to his seat half open so I could climb in. However, I ignored him, he said, and calmly crawled up front with the driver.

He seemed quite nice. Don't know whether he was especially impressed with me. (Only married men seem to be thoroughly appreciative.)

The matchmaker instinct in Erma is strong. She's already arranged to have me come over tomorrow night to play cards, and Charlie will be there.

Wednesday, February 11, 1931

Friday night I went over to play cards as arranged and Charlie was there. We played until about 10:30 and then I went up to the roundhouse with him while he let his locomotive engine build up steam. He came on home with me then and made a fire. It was 1:30 a.m. before he left.

I like him very much but don't know whether we can make a "go" of it, because he's been around a lot and has different standards than I do. He couldn't see my point of view, but I guess we came to some agreement in the end. By telling him that I wouldn't change *ever* and that he'd better not come back if he expected a different type, I showed him how I felt, but I also told him that I'd be sorry if I didn't see him again.

Then he said he'd come around again and *wouldn't* ask me to go against my conscience. He quizzed me about my love life—past and present—and drew a blank, of course. While we were at the Christensens, he asked me to go to a dance next week since Mike suggested we make a foursome and go. (Good old Mike, the matchmaker.)

Sunday, February 15, 1931

Another experience. Last night my date to go dancing flopped because Charlie simply failed to show up. At first I was dreadfully humiliated, but now I don't feel quite so angry and disillusioned. I'm beginning to believe that it was for the best. He is so attractive and so persuasively argues that morality and immorality are merely matters of opinion that he is hard to resist. I felt hopelessly prudish and was unable to come up with one blessed reason why I shouldn't let him have his way. All I could do was stubbornly reiterate that I wasn't that kind of a girl. (All that he said didn't sound crude because he is a smooth talker and somehow seems refined, no matter what he is saying.)

Finally, before he left, he said he'd never bother me under any circumstances and several times during the evening remarked that I was "interesting." In other words, different from the cookhouse flunkies and girls he met when he was in the navy. It is now pretty plain, though, that he prefers a more cooperative kind of girl even if she isn't so novel and "interesting."

It humiliated me to be left waiting, but when I saw how "sunk" poor Mike and Erma were to have their protege act that way, I started cheering them up. With all sincerity I told them it was probably for the best because Charlie might have turned out to be a bit too much for me to handle.

They took me to a show in St. Helens that evening and when they brought me home, they came in. Mike made a fire for me, and they stayed and visited until 12:30. Mike said, "Now look here, little girl, you stick to your ideals and you'll never be sorry. There are good guys running around though they are hard to find."

I am in complete agreement with that last statement. This whole business is like a matching test we give in geography. On one side of the page is a list of cities and across from them a column with the names of the most important product from each city. These, however, are not in correct order. The problem is to match each city with the correct product.

But the trouble is that in life there are no neat columns of just the right number of men and women to choose from. When you are out to find a matching man in life, it is a grand scramble to meet *anyone*, and then when he invariably doesn't match you, it becomes discouraging. There must be some way to meet someone who is fairly attractive, interesting, and also decent. I don't demand a saint—only someone who likes me for myself, not what he can get out of me. If all a man appreciates about you is that you are the right sex, you might just as well as a frowzy moron.

February 8, 1931
Newest development and the last. I stopped in
to ask Erma what excuse Charlie had given for his
nonappearance Saturday night. We all thought
the excuse about his suit not being back from the
cleaners was rather feeble and did not show much
imagination.

One thing that Charlie said, though, makes me
think that it was some kind of a recommendation—Mike was kidding him by saying, "Now
don't you get hard with Grace because I promised
her mother I'd protect her from these rough loggers," to which Charlie replies, "Don't worry,
you have to *pay* for her." Mike, of course, asked
him what he meant by that, and Charlie answered,
"Yes, you pay for her with a wedding ring."

That restores my self-respect because I see that
he understood what I was talking about. Give the
boy credit, though, he has the strength of his
convictions. He wanted a woman who would give
him his way, so he would not appear even at the
probability of peeving Mike.

Despite the lack of a party telephone line, there must have been
some way that people in the logging camp kept tab on what others
were doing. At least it would seem so, because I had never mentioned Charlie's name to Mary and yet:

February 24, 1931
My latest report on the man named Charlie—
Mary Troy said she had been so worried that I
might go with him because he has a terrible
reputation. He is keeping a woman in Portland
and almost everyone out here knows it. Am I ever
thankful that I never went any place with him!

Still, what makes me peeved is that, although
Mike knew what sort Charlie was, he still brought
him to see me. I suppose there might be a slim
chance that he didn't know all about him, but
from what I hear, loggers talk over *all* their
concerns in a thorough manner, and since Mike
worked with Charlie, it seems likely that he'd
heard about the mistress lurking in the background.

Today, while I was walking up by the cookhouse, Charlie's engine went by. I couldn't think of any appropriate expression to assume when I saw him, but since he was leaning out of the cab window beaming on me, I settled for a faint smile. Maybe I'm fooling myself, but I believe that he respected me and decided that since I was such an obstinate idealist, he'd let me be that way. At least I *hope* that is the way he felt.

That same day I also had the following to report:
This forenoon Erma came up during school time to say goodbye. Mike had become angry with his boss and quit his job. They were already packed and on their way, so I went out to their car to talk for a minute. Too bad to have such a temper in these hard times when it's not a snap to get a job any more.

I guess Clarke Wilson is cutting the wages all the time. Anyway I heard Mike tell Charlie that he wasn't going to break *his* neck getting more logs loaded on the trains. "Not for any measly four dollars a day." I wonder if he realizes how scarce jobs are. I do hope they can keep up the payments for the insurance premiums, stocks, etc.

It made me sad and lonesome to go past their house this afternoon and see how deserted it looked standing there empty.

I did not see or hear of the Christensens again until two years later when I encountered Erma in a Portland bus depot. She told me that Mike was working away from home in a logging camp in Washington, but as we talked, I sensed that they had seen some lean times after they left Wilark. When I asked about their investments, she said they had lost everything, but she did not appear downhearted. Erma had been blessed with an optimistic and even temperament so perhaps she was counting on the good years that so often follow the bad ones. Right then she was so pleased to show me their baby daughter that nothing else mattered.

7

All of my girl friends' husbands were employed when I saw them during the fall of 1930, but as the Depression deepened, I began to see its effects upon their lives. When Frank Tacheron lost his good-paying position as a salesman, he and Mable moved to a small suburban acreage. There Frank raised a garden and kept a cow and chickens while Mable did her part by canning and preserving the surplus food he grew. She had lived in the country as a youngster and knew how to make butter and cottage cheese so she was able to bring in cash by delivering these and loaves of her homemade bread to regular customers in their neighborhood.

The Tacherons practiced every economy that they had ever heard of and discovered new ones. They used newspapers to cover the bare boards of the attic bedroom where their older son Bobby slept. For several months before he entered school, Bobby studied the pictures and headlines displayed on the walls until he became familiar with the letters of the alphabet. As soon as his first grade teacher taught him some phonetical clues to unlocking words, he was on his way to independent reading. I thought that Mable was an almost unnaturally modest mother when she gave the credit for his good progress to the newspapered walls rather than to genetics.

But back to the economies which became so much a part of my friends' lives during those years—I remember noticing how warmly dressed the little boys were in the mackinaws which Mable made over from men's woolen overcoats. Maybe they had been Frank's but could have been resurrected from a trunk in some relative's attic. Mable was proud that she had devised a way to make warm mittens out of a pair of a man's old woolen socks, and she also made dresses for herself out of the garments that she had discarded in better times. This was necessary because, in spite of the

Depression, styles regarding skirt lengths steadily changed. Hemlines dropped from the knees or above in 1928 to just below the calf of the leg by 1932.

Members of the Tacheron family brushed their teeth with Arm and Hammer soda instead of toothpaste, and to take the place of a fancy hand lotion, Mable, who had been Franklin High School's dainty May Day Queen in 1922, now saved the whey when she made cottage cheese and used that on her work-worn hands.

A welfare program was finally instituted in 1932 so Frank was able to get work on a road-construction project, but never having worked as a manual laborer before, he was not enthusiastic about his job. When he told us about being ordered to move faster so he could haul more loads of dirt with a wheelbarrow, it was plain that he was finding it hard to swallow his pride and obey orders, but he did because it was the only paid employment available.

I noticed library books scattered around the house every time I went there. From his remarks, I gathered that Frank was delving into socialism and communism, but this did not seem startling because there was no strong anti-communism sentiment in the United States at that time. He was not the only one who was questioning the merits of a capitalistic system under which a complete economic breakdown could occur. Those who were interested pursued their studies of different ideologies, including communism, quite openly.

My recollections of what my friends did to weather the troubled times are sketchy, and probably I have not conveyed the good spirits with which they met the challenge. Perhaps they maintained their courage because they knew that most of the other couples in their social group were having similar experiences, and as they listened to the radio they realized that they were just one family out of millions who were undergoing hardships, either as bad as theirs or incomparably worse.

The fortunate people during the Depression were those who were employed by railroads, utility companies, or some government agency, including school districts that could sell their warrants. I was employed by one of those districts and knew that I was very lucky.

> March 26,1931
>
> I realize that I should be very grateful when I hear of the hard times with so many people unable to get work, and even of the hardships of some of the family men out here in camp who are working for less than one hundred dollars a month. Here I am with $140 per month, and almost $130 of that is clear because there are no rent, fuel, or water bills to pay, and my half of the grocery bill never exceeds ten dollars.
>
> January 4, 1932
>
> How lucky I am! Here I sit with this job at $140 a month while people everywhere are without jobs. The worst of it is that if a man loses his job, that's it—there's no hope of finding another one.
>
> Right now I have $420 in my savings account, warrants from Stanfield still to be cashed, and $700 yet to come in from my teaching this year. I'm grateful and make no mistake.

Being one of the two highest paid rural teachers in the county gave me satisfaction in more ways than one. One incident which brought about this satisfaction occurred after my friend, Mary Dippert, who had taken me under her wing in Clatskanie, introduced me to one of her acquaintances.

> A St. Helens teacher tried to patronize me at the County Institute last week. As soon as she heard Mary say that I was teaching in Wilark (out in the country), she said a bit too sweetly, "That's nice. I suppose you are out there trying to gather some years of experience."
>
> Then Mary hastily intercepted with, "Oh, but Grace likes to teach in a country school. She likes it better than in town."
>
> I couldn't resist casually remarking, "Yes, and I confess that the pay appeals to me."

The woman was simply pop-eyed when she had finished cross-examining me about the financial rewards out here. She even murmured feebly that she'd always wanted to teach in a rural school. That was something radically different for a town teacher to say to a country school teacher. Money makes the difference!

For various reasons my previous plans to return to college were set aside that year. One was that life now held more entertainment for me, so I no longer craved a change as I had at Stanfield.

A second reason was that I needed to save additional money before I could spend a year on the University of Oregon campus, and I could not save money and also give in to my weakness for pretty clothes.

March 10, 1931

Spring clothes are beginning to haunt me. I can't decide whether or not to buy a suit. They are adorable this year.

April 26, 1931

I must record that I weakened when I was in Portland last Saturday. I bought a red knit dress and a hat to match. The dress fits me like my silk-and-wool winter underwear, and by *that* I mean snugly revealing a few slender curves. The hat and dress complete the outfit which my blue suede jacket began when I bought it a couple of months ago.

On those Saturday forenoons when I wandered through Portland's stores, I often saw tempting merchandise on display. I shall never forget the navy blue broadcloth coat with its silver-gray astrakan fur collar I bought that fall. Without a doubt it was the finest coat I have ever had. Not only was it beautifully tailored and chic-looking but the materials were the best. For this luxurious garment I paid sixty-nine depression-time dollars but the saleslady assured me that I was getting a bargain because it was marked down from eighty-nine dollars. I have no idea what such a coat would cost nowadays, but I am certain that if the fur collar were in style now, it alone would cost many times what I paid for the coat in 1931.

After having just finished my account of the financial trials and tribulations of the country as a whole, and my friends in particular, it makes me feel guilty to write about the additions I made to my wardrobe during those years. I am reminded of Nero fiddling while Rome burned or Marie Antoinette suggesting that the starving peasants eat cake since they had no bread. In fact, I thought that it might be wise to ignore the subject until it dawned on me that, except for the sixty-nine dollar coat, I had not been extravagant. Prices were so low that it did not cost much to be well dressed. For instance, the soft suede-leather jacket, which was a delightfully vivid violet-blue color, was priced at sixteen dollars because it was of a much finer quality than those on the nine-dollar rack.

There were other reasons for my failure to add money to my savings account that year.

November 26, 1930

Next Friday is payday but I won't be able to put anything in savings because the folks need to pay their taxes. There is no demand for potatoes this year, and that's the crop they planted in the hopes that it would bring in some money for this winter. I guess it behooves me to produce the tax money. I owe on my coat too. Oh well, I've decided that I won't go to college next year, so there's not so much need to be frugal.

I had discontinued my practice of sending money home each month after I had reimbursed my parents for the expense of my first year at normal school, but they knew that they could depend on my financial help whenever there was an emergency. Then too, there were other ways that I could be of help. I gave the paint for the outside of the farmhouse as a Christmas present one year, and paint and paper for its interior one other time. I paid for my younger sister's piano lessons (fifty cents per lesson) and helped provide clothes for my mother and sister, either by purchasing new ones for them, or giving them my too-short garments. Maybe I did more, but this is enough to take me feel less guilty about buying an elegant blue broadcloth coat when so many women were wearing outmoded or made-over garments.

8

March 26, 1931

Monday night Esther and I took the blank unsigned contracts that Mr. Stendal had given us a long time ago back up to him so he could fill them out. I guess they had already rehired us, because Mr. Stendal immediately filled them in and signed his name in the proper place on the contracts, and we did too, so now that's taken care of.

In passing, I must jubilantly add that next year's salary will be the same as this year's—no cut in salary!

We were hired for another year but we didn't rest on our laurels because we knew that with such good pay we had to do out best so people would think we deserved it.

Mr. Baker, being Superintendent of Logging Operations for the Clarke Wilson Lumber Company, was by far the most important person in Wilark. Although his own children attended Portland schools, it was a matter of pride with him that the youngsters in this headquarters' camp be given an opportunity for a good education, so he encouraged the company-controlled school board members to attract competent teachers by paying tempting salaries and to provide the school with the best available equipment. In return for this generosity, he expected other districts to be made aware that Wilark had a good school.

Elizabeth Murray knew he felt that way so when she dropped by after school one day, she advised me to have handicrafts from Wilark School be entered for competition at the Columbia County Fair the following September. This meant that anything the youngsters might enter at the fair would have to be made before school closed.

After I found out the type of articles the fair officials wanted, I talked to my youngsters and we decided to have all the upper grade boys become members of a 4-H Woodworking Club. I would act as leader and all the materials would be paid for by the school district, with tools being brought by the boys from home.

The 4-H Woodworking Handbook had patterns to follow so we went into action with meetings from 2:00 to 4:00 every Friday afternoon. In the meantime the girls were at Mrs. Hewett's house where she was acting as leader of their 4-H Sewing Club.

Of course I was of no practical help to my charges but I could sit on one end of a board to steady it as the boys sawed and I gave them moral support and encouragement.

They made birdhouses and a number of other articles, many of which were not fit to be sent to the fair, but some were quite good. The girls prepared samples of their sewing for display and both the upper and lower grade rooms were preparing art work to be exhibited. That was when the excellent creative art class I had taken during the summer of 1928 paid off at Wilark.

May 5, 1931
We're working on material for the fair. Such a cutting and pasting goes on! Every evening the rooms look as if a hurricane had passed through. Even if we don't win any prizes, we hope the school board will be pleased that we made the effort.

We fared better than I had hoped. Wilark school children took so many prizes that Mr. Baker (who attended the fair) accused Elizabeth of bribing the judges in Wilark's behalf. That was really rather amusing, because the only reason the youngsters took first, second, and third prizes in some instances was that Wilark was the only school with entries in that category. In other words, there was no competition.

During the spring so many families were transferred to other camps that I had only fourteen pupils left. But some of those who remained would be taking the state tests.

On May 14th the crucial day had arrived.

Today and tomorrow are exam days. Gosh! I
hate to think of looking over three of the pupils'
papers. They are some of the most poorly
prepared children I've ever had. But I can be
grateful that one other slow one has moved away.
I won't have to be depressed by his papers too.

June 16, 1931
(At home on the farm)

I closed school O.K. Thanks to Elizabeth's
friendship all of my poor pupils were allowed to
pass out of the eight grade. It was the only
sensible thing to do because they never would be
able to do it on their own ability. On Saturday,
the day after school was out, I had to go to the
graduation exercises for the eighth graders.

The matter-of-fact statement about Elizabeth's "passing" my
low-achieving pupils in spite of their failing test papers shows that
my attitude toward state examinations had changed considerably
through the years. At Midland I was shocked by the unethical
behavior of one of my predecessors who had helped her pupils
answer test questions. During my two years at Stanfield I lost some
more of my starry-eyed idealism. I saw that the upper grade
teacher in a nearby town maintained her excellent teaching
reputation by a more subtle means than simply giving the pupils
the answers to test questions. At Wilark confrontations with
belligerent parents had shown me that a teacher—especially a
seventh and eighth grade teacher—often received the blame for a
child's lack of success in school. It was possible for a youngster to
enter the upper grades totally unprepared, having been passed on
from grade to grade. Then by some miracle, the upper grade
teacher was supposed to fill in all the gaps so the child could pass
the state tests.

Yes, I was more realistic after five years of teaching. I wasn't
upset by the possibility that Elizabeth might have graded my pupils
more leniently because she was my friend. I knew she often gave
passing grades to hopelessly slow students, so I did not concern
myself with the ethical aspects. I was just thankful that none of
Wilark's youngsters had been failed.

A day-long celebration honoring all the graduating eighth graders in Columbia County was held at St. Helens each spring. There was a parade in the forenoon in which each group of teacher and pupils joined all the other school groups to walk through streets lined with town folk, and anyone else who happened to be there. It was a long, hot walk in the late spring sunshine so we were glad to arrive at the Methodist Church and be served a free meal by the Ladies' Aid Society. We ended up at the county courthouse where each graduate received his eighth grade diploma, carefully rolled and tied with a silk ribbon.

This document was to be valued and preserved because it proved that the pupil had fulfilled all the state requirements for compulsory education, and for some children it marked the end of their school days.

In June I again enrolled in the University of Oregon Extension Summer School at Lincoln High School in Portland. I signed up for classes in Oregon History, State Government, and Correlation of Subject Matter, for which I paid the usual tuition fee of twenty dollars.

I stayed with my friend Louise who lived in a rooming house which at one time had been an elegant dwelling but was now run-down and shabby. However, there still were a few reminders of its more prosperous days: the stationary marble washbasin, the beautifully-carved staircase, and the parlor's elaborate gas light fixture which was still in place beside the currently used electric light. Of most interest to me was the button-bell at the head of our bed which long ago had been pressed to summon a maid to milady's boudoir.

The summer was an unusually hot one, so the rooming house did not cool off from one day to the next. To avoid studying in my room, I spent the afternoons in the Lincoln High School library or went to Portland's Central Library which was less than a block from my residence. My diary mentions such temperatures as 102° at 10 p.m. but we were young so slept soundly in spite of the heat and the noisy streetcars that passed below our open windows.

Following summer school was a short stay on the farm before I left for the coast where I would be the guest of Ethel Fenwick whom I had visited in Klamath Falls during the previous Christmas season. She and her mother had rented a beach cabin at Bandon, Oregon, which was then a twelve hour bus ride from Portland.

During the ensuing two weeks Ethel and I walked along the beach searching for agates, sunbathed on the sand, and best of all enjoyed the cool sea breezes after having sweltered in the hot inland temperatures all summer. And we found other ways to be entertained.

We went to two dances. At the first one we met a couple of men from Heppner who are at the coast on business. When I say "men," I mean it. They were not kids (more nearly forty is my guess), but the one I was with was a good dancer and really nice and respectful. His abject admiration for me reminded me of Lloyd at Summer Lake.

Ethel's mother was shocked and protested because we were going out with men we'd met at a dance, but we let them take us deep-sea fishing in spite of her dire predictions. My escort tried to make plans for looking me up in Portland next winter, but I have a sneaking suspicion that there's a wife in the background. Even if I were interested (which I'm not), nothing would come of his plans. When he gets back home under his wife's thumb (*if she does exist*), he will cast all of those naughty thoughts about cheating on her out of his mind.

SECOND YEAR AT WILARK 1931-1932

Esther and I spent the weekend prior to the first day of school in 1931 donating our services. We were working with textbooks so the district would be in compliance with a new law that required public schools to provide free textbooks to elementary school children. Our pupils had turned in all their books when school closed in May, so we had those to process as well as some newly-purchased ones.

Following the instructions sent out by the county school superintendent's office, we cleaned the outside of the used books by sponging them off with a cloth dipped in water containing Lysol. After they dried, we applied two coats of shellac to both the old and the new textbooks and finally stamped each one, "Property of District Number 43, Columbia County, Oregon."

As we went through all these steps, we had the assistance of Mrs. Plum, the new school clerk. I had been pleasantly surprised when she showed up to help us, for we had never met her before, and I impulsively decided that she was one of those generous souls who go around looking for a way to be of service. I should have known better, because it was she who had requested us to shorten our vacation so we could work on the books without pay. Later, when we handed in the school supply order, I was further convinced that she was anything but generous.

Mrs. George Plum III, as she signs herself, is Wilark's new school clerk. She doesn't forget for a minute that her husband is related to one of the owners of the Clarke Wilson Lumber Company, so she loyally attempts to curb school costs, which in turn will reduce the company's school taxes. And besides, displaying her authority as a school clerk probably provides her with a new interest since she's young and there isn't much for her to do in camp.

But what a jolt she is after Mr. Stendal's easygoing attitude! She carefully examines each request before reluctantly giving her approval. Oh well, so far the only drastic changes have been that we now pay five dollars apiece toward the house rent and no longer receive free firewood.

On September 13, 1931, I had finished the first week of my sixth year as a teacher.

Five years ago today (September 13, 1926) I taught my first day of school at Summer Lake. How thrilled I was but also fully aware that teaching those four youngsters was going to be quite a responsibility.

I'd heard Grandpa Dustin tell of opening the school year by making a little speech to his pupils, so that is what I tried to do. I remember that my voice quavered even though I was addressing such a small number of pupils—only four children. How could I ever forget?

Professionally, I'm not much farther today than I was then, but in my personal development I believe I have made progress. I've acquired some poise and self-confidence and gathered many friends along the way.

Since Wilark's school population is up again after last spring's exodus from camp, I'm starting the year with a roomful. So is Esther. So far these youngsters seem to be easier to handle than last year's batch. For one thing, they aren't so mature for their age. No big, overgrown boys and the

112

girls are less quarrelsome and better behaved. Of course they are all trying me out to see what they can get by with—how little work and how much play I'll tolerate during school time.

Two days of last week were County Institute days. All the talk was "Hard Times," "Retrenchment," cuts in salary, etc. Everybody knows that these are desperately difficult times, but they'll be more so for teachers if they have their salaries cut and still have to live three months out of the year without pay.

All Alone, Friday, Oct. 23, 1931

I've signed up for a four-hour credit correspondence course—Survey of American Literature—from the University of Oregon which should keep me busy this winter. This weekend I thought I'd spend every minute working, but I've wasted this first evening lying here on the couch, sleeping, reading, listening to the radio, and playing with our kitten, David, named after David the Giant Killer. We brought him out here in the hopes that he would grow up and be a match for the packrats that disturb our peace of mind and sense of smell. The pests are noisy overhead and give the house a bad odor even though they can't get into our rooms. They are in the attic and reminders of them come in the form of liquid drippings which fall on the floor, chairs, tables, or whatever happens to be under a crack or knothole in the ceiling. Oh, ye pioneer experience!

Sunday, October 25, 1931

Only two days since I last wrote, but I thought I'd report on how I've fared. I worked like a good girl this weekend—washing clothes, scrubbed the floors, corrected a pile of papers, made out report cards, and worked on the correspondence course. There wasn't much time left to feel bored.

I also went over to Mary's on Saturday afternoon and stayed to dinner since I was to consider it my birthday dinner. Boy! All kidding aside—I'm hating that quarter of a century mark.

I told Mary that I had been concentrating on the thought that I was still twenty-four, and then she rudely rushes to celebrate my twenty-fifth birthday two weeks ahead of time.

Since my weekend passed so quickly, I'm more convinced than ever that I'll stay in camp often this year. Visiting Mary in the afternoon shortens the day so I don't mind the evenings here alone with my kitty and a warm fire while the rain beats down on (and sometimes through) the roof.

Armistice Day (no school)
November 11, 1931

Here we are again. One quarter of a century has passed since I was born. Oh golly! Year after year goes past and I'm not keeping up with the grand parade, it seems. This morning I woke up before daybreak and started thinking about life and how it is rushing by. I tried to reason with myself but in spite of everything I felt punk.

I suppose that these years are serving a purpose and that someday I may look back longingly to my present freedom, youth, and good salary. The way things look now, I won't be worrying about having no freedom because, for sure, that is one thing that isn't threatened.

The mood did not persist, however, because the rest of the account of that day tells that Esther and I waxed floors, bathed the cat with Lux soap, dropped in to see our pupils' friendly mothers on our way to and from the commissary, and shared the "pretty good" dinner I cooked that evening.

As a potential defender of our household, David turned out to be a disappointment. He was a sickly cat in spite of the care which we lavished on him, so Esther took him back to the farm. We then decided that it would be more practical to complain to Jimmy Troy about the unwelcome tenants in our attic.

He called the matter to the attention of the maintenance department, but it was understaffed because there was a policy to do little or no repair work on the camp houses which would soon be abandoned when camp was moved to another site. Finally after I'd complained to Jimmy several more times, a workman did arrive and crawled into our attic through the trapdoor in the kitchen ceiling. He sprinkled poison around and when he came down, he spoke with wonder of the skeltons of previously poisoned rats that he had seen up there. He told us that some were sixteen inches in length. How glad we were that there was no way that the varmints could get into our living quarters! Also we were grateful to the present generation for going out into the woods to die after they obligingly swallowed the poison that the man put in the attic.

There was one other time that fall when we appealed to Jimmy for help in getting some action out of the maintenance department. That was when our roof leaked. Our requests for repairs had been ignored until the situation was almost desperate.

> The roof is leaking worse than usual. Dishpans, kettles, the bedchamber (for the leak behind the bedroom door, of course), washpans, etc., are scattered around to catch the water that dribbles out of the ceiling. Then when a drip fell on my pillow all one night, that was just too much because in that tiny room there's no place to move the bed.

The morning after my drip-troubled night, I sent a note by one of the children to Jimmy telling him about the containers scattered around (all except the one behind the bedroom door) and added that the reason for my unusual desperation was the drip on my pillow. I ended up by telling him that I was confidently waiting for him to demonstrate his executive ability in our behalf. He passed the note around for Mr. Baker, camp superintendent, and the rest of the men in the office to see. After reading it, they all agreed that a drip falling on one's pillow could indeed be unusually annoying. Then Mr. Baker unbent enough to disregard the austerity program and good-naturedly said, "I guess we can't have the teachers losing their sleep, Jim, so you'd better see about getting someone to fix their roof."

And so, for the rest of that year we lived happily in a dry house.

115

2

In September I wrote:
> I'm almost convinced that I may be economical
> this winter. I didn't go into Portland last weekend
> and here I am staying out in camp again. If
> college is goal for next year, I must skimp and
> pinch every penny.

I had suddenly realized that my younger sister, a junior in high school, would soon be needing my financial help to go to normal school. Therefore, it behooved me to go to college before that time arrived. So I made out a budget:

Living expenses (food, rent, fuel)	$ 20
Savings	80
Incidental expenses	
(clothing, bus fares, gifts, gifts, etc.)	40
Total	$140

A few weeks later a savings and loan company salesman looked me up with the purpose of persuading me to pay into an investment plan with his firm. When I explained that I intended to use my savings for college the following year, he assured me that would be no problem. The amount I invested could be withdrawn by merely giving thirty days' notice. Since I had already decided to save an additional ten dollars each month, I agreed to put that much money into the investment plan because it paid 6% interest which was higher than the 4% banks paid.

This extra ten dollars had to be taken out of the amount budgeted for "incidentals" but I generally ignored this fact and used my charge account when I saw something I wanted to buy.

Two weeks ago when Mary and I were shopping together in Portland, we came across a fabulous bargain in good-looking chairs for only twenty dollars. It was too good to resist, so I bought a Cogswell chair upholstered in tapestry for Mama's and Papa's Christmas present. Charged it to my account—naturally.

Prices were incredibly low so I found myself buying gifts for people not ordinarily on my Christmas list. For Mary I bought two presents, a music box and some earrings she'd admired, because she had made me a flattering floor length dinner dress out of the velvet material I'd purchased one day when we were shopping together. As I heedlessly charged purchases to my account at Meier and Frank and Company, I was sure that it was better to give than to receive, but when the bills started to come in after the holidays, I began to have some doubts.

January 13, 1932

I have a fifty-seven dollar bill at Meier-Frank's thanks to my Christmas splurge.

I'm going home this weekend on the Friday evening bus and have Papa meet me at the end of the streetcar line that night. If I do that, I'll not be tempted to buy things in Portland as I am when I wait and go in on the Saturday morning bus. Goodness knows, though, I'm in no position to spend money because I have only $1.53 in my checking account, about five dollars in cash, and it's two weeks until payday.

February 2, 1932

Much excitement when I studied my cancelled checks and bank statement and discovered that I would be overdrawn if all outstanding checks were cashed. I therefore had to write a note posthaste to Jimmy at the commissary to tell him to hold that last check which I'd written to Esther and he had cashed for her.

March 11, 1932

No new clothes until next payday. I still owe Meier-Frank thirty-five dollars. Curse my generosity at Christmas!

To be quite honest, I must admit that all my indebtedness could not be blamed on what I bought for others. I was buying clothes that would be suitable for college, so when I saw an especially good bargain, I added that to my charge account.

When I began to hear of the epidemic of bank failures all over the nation, I decided to take my savings out of a bank in downtown Portland and put them into a United States postal savings account. While I was at the bank, I also closed my checking account. How tightly I clutched my purse as I carried the four hundred dollars in currency over to the Pioneer Post Office! The postal savings account paid only one percent interest compared to the three percent paid by banks, but that was unimportant compared to the fact that my account had the backing of the United States Government.

On my way out to the farm I opened a checking account at the small suburban bank where my parents had theirs.

3

For the first two months of the school year there were a few normally mischievous boys in my room but no one to worry me to any extent. That pleasant state of affairs ended when Clifford enrolled in November. From the first day I knew that he was going to be a challenge, not because of his size or age, for he was an undersized sixth grader, but because of his qualities of leadership. He led the rest of the boys into all sorts of scrapes. One day, for example, they all went out into the woods on the edge of the schoolground, and although the bell to resume afternoon classes could be heard for half a mile, they ignored it and stayed out an additional half hour. For several weeks the playground was as violent as it had been the previous year because Clifford had organized his classmates into rival gangs.

Still, I shall never forget the time he used his gifts in behalf of a fifth grade girl from Trenholm. One morning as she came into the classroom wearing glasses for the first time, I saw that she had been fitted with old-fashioned steel-framed spectacles. She was surrounded by teasing classmates and was crying. This was not the first time she had been teased. She had a speech defect, and being a

Grace Brandt in front of playshed at Wilark

foster child whose keep was paid for by the county, she always was poorly dressed and neglected looking. Instead of feeling sorry for her, the rest of the children delighted in making fun of her.

I took her on my lap and told the children who had followed her to my desk how cruel they were to make the little girl feel bad about something for which she was not to blame. I was repeating what I'd said on other occasions when they teased her, but this time my words had the desired effect. Clifford listened to my plea for kindness and took it to heart. When he and his henchmen went outside, he let them know that they were not to mention the glasses again. They didn't and the girls in our room followed their example.

Another lasting memory of Clifford has to do with the night we put on the traditional Christmas program which was attended by most of the people in camp, including the single loggers who lived in bunkhouses. Clifford had the leading role in the upper grade

119

play, so it was a small tragedy to have him turn up for the performance half-drunk. Being inexperienced in such matters, I didn't know what to do, but some of my better informed pupils agreed that leading him around in the cold drizzle would soon make him sober. Two of them, carrying their flashlights, led Clifford around and around the schoolhouse until they considered him fit to go on stage.

The Christmas program started a bit late that year, but Clifford had the instincts of a true trouper for he rallied and no one in the audience suspected that our boy hero had sampled his parents' bootleg liquor that evening. Although our school clerk commented on Mrs. Santa Claus chewing a wad of gum throughout the play, she had nothing unfavorable to say about Clifford's performance.

Every once in a while Clifford's little sister, who was in the first grade, would tell Esther that her mother was away from home. From the camp gossip we'd heard, we surmised that the children's mother must be in Portland again, going to a round of drinking parties. Sometimes she would stay away for over a week, leaving her husband and three children to fend for themselves. So I understood that there was a good reason for my pupil's disturbing behavior and I was sorry that he had to live in such a home atmosphere, but nevertheless, I was elated when his father was transferred to another camp.

Monday, April 17, 1932

Back again to begin the thirty-second week of school. But here, my good diary, is the difference: Clifford's father has been moved! This means that no more can Clifford lead my normally well-behaved boys astray. As I told Esther, I feel as if I've been granted five extra weeks of vacation now that he is out of the picture.

4

Because the correspondence course I was taking had to be completed by June, I spent many weekends in Wilark studying about American literature. When I did leave, however, I found that my weekends away from camp were completely different from those of the preceding year.

In the first place, Louise had moved to a studio apartment which she shared with a girl from her hometown. They had only one bed which folded down out of a wall closet, so when I was an overnight guest, it made a crowded three-to-a-bed situation. I could understand why the other girl didn't appreciate being inconvenienced by a stranger, so I stayed there just two times, which was one time too many.

Therefore, most of the time I rode into Portland on the Saturday morning bus from Wilark and then went on out to the farm.

> When I first get home, Mama and Papa sit and
> beam at their wandering child as she tells of her
> troubles and triumphs since the last time they saw
> her. Mama's lap is a trifle small for me nowadays,
> but it makes me feel completely "un-Miss Brandt-
> ish" as I sit there, feeling their sympathetic in-
> terest in everything that I am telling them.

How many memories that passage from my diary brings to mind!

When the weather was pleasant, I went horseback riding with my sister Clarice. Our mounts were the two farm horses my father used when he plowed and cultivated the fields. Clarice rode the livelier of the two, while it was my lot to ride Nig, whose hooves were the size of dinner plates. When Lady broke into a trot, I encouraged Nig to follow suit. If he did, it was a strange experience because mysterious rumbling sounds came from his insides as he laboriously and unrhythmically bounded over the ground. In spite of all the drawbacks I had a good time.

> Monday was Washington's Birthday so I spent
> the afternoon riding with Clarice. We went
> through people's pastures, opening and closing

gates along the way, and finally started crossing logged-off land until we came out on the hill above Boring. Below us were all the valley lands with neat red barns and trim white houses set in the squares of farmland. Above it we could see the snow peaks, Mt. Hood, Mt. St. Helens, and Mt. Adams, all linked together by snow-covered foothills. Clarice and I got off the horses and sat in the sunlight, enjoying the view and the quietness.

Clarice Brandt and Grace Brandt, attired in daytime pajamas, so popular in 1931 and 1932.

More and more frequently I was the guest of Sylvia and Leib Riggs who had been my friends four years ago (1927-28) when I was teaching at Midland. They then were newly married and both were graduates of the School of Pharmacy at Oregon State College. Their drugstore's food counter in Clatskanie was a gathering place for the young unmarried teachers and single professional men in town. Instead of remaining at Midland, I had spent most of my weekends in Clatskanie with my friend, Mary Dippert, who taught there. So, through her I became acquainted with the Riggs and found Sylvia, with her quick wit, a delightful companion.

In 1931 the young couple sold their pharmacy in Clatskanie and bought a larger one in Hillsboro which was close to Portland. When I visited them that year Sylvia always met me at the bus depot in Portland on Friday evening and took me back there in time to catch the Sunday evening bus for Wilark.

October 18, 1931

I went to Hillsboro to see the Riggs last weekend. Sylvia was being artistic as she arranged the furniture in the new house they are moving into. We shoved pieces of furniture around in various places, and then she would drop her head to one side and critically survey the effect through half-closed eyes. We carried boxes up and down stairs, ironed drapes, and looked hours on end for the pushpins so we could hang up the tapestry. The thought of them was in the back of our minds all day until it got so we'd flinch whenever we heard the word "pushpins." I also helped put the rug under the dining room table and on and on, but it was fun and gave me some ideas about furniture arrangement.

January 4, 1932

Happy New Year, my dear young lady! How my heart throbs with sincerity as I make that wish for myself.

Over the holidays I went out to visit the Riggs. Sylvia gave a bridge party in my honor. It was a pleasant evening with several of the socially-minded ladies from the community competing for first prize. As usual, I did not shine at the card table, so in addition to a pair of house slippers which Sylvia gave to me as the guest of honor, I received the booby prize (a can of sauerkraut juice).

New Year's Eve offered varied attractions. During the course of the evening, we dropped in on some of their friends, and later a group of us went to a midnight matinee. We finally ended up making merry in the Riggs' party room from 2:30 a.m. until 4 a.m. By that time most of the people were feeling pretty happy, thanks to the liquor served at the party.

On New Year's Day we ate breakfast at 1:30 p.m. and spent the rest of the afternoon planting tulip and daffodil bulbs. That evening Sylvia and I went to another movie which was a dumb cowboy affair.

Saturday morning, in a grand finale, I made it in just fifty minutes from the time I climbed out of bed until I was seated (with hat askew) in the bus.

May 1, 1932

Just back from another visit to the Riggs. Sylvia and Leib met me in Portland Friday evening and on our way out to Hillsboro, Leib stopped the car on Terwilliger Boulevard so we could look out over the city's lights. He bought some Karmelcorn earlier so we munched on that as we enjoyed the view.

Saturday night we went to the midnight matinee because Leib doesn't close the drug store until nine o'clock. Afterwards Sylvia had two couples, including the town social leader and her husband, come back to the house for a bite to eat and something with a kick in it to drink. (Much hilarity characterized the evening.)

The lady is reputed to be very jealous, so when her husband glanced at me pleasantly during the evening, I looked at him in a kindly, school teacher manner. I guess that convinced her that I was harmless, because the next morning she brought over some lilacs for me to take back to Wilark.

I loved to be with Sylvia because she made a lark out of whatever we were doing together. She bolstered my self-esteem by complimenting me on whatever talents I had, and to my surprise, envied me my tall, slim figure. I discovered that Sylvia not only had the faculty for being a boon companion, but possessed the ability to influence people to her way of thinking. While at her place, I found myself smoking cigarettes as we lingered at the table after eating, and on other occasions also. At their lively parties I drank little or no liquor because I disliked the taste of alcohol, but I was wholly tolerant of others who did, even the one or two who might drink to excess.

While talking to my family about these weekends, I always left out the parts about the alcoholic drinks at parties, and I was just as reticent about my smoking. Nevertheless, my mother guessed that being with Sylvia was causing a change in me so she deplored our friendship. While I was at home though, she kept her opinion to herself. It was through Clarice that I learned of her concern.

My mother and I did not see eye to eye on a great many subjects. We often disagreed, yet we loved one another. I also respected her because I knew she was intelligent and, in many ways, wise. I realized that as far as her children were concerned, she was especially vulnerable, so I could not bear the thought of hurting her and my father by adopting ways that did not meet with their expectations for me. As a consequence, without its being too much of a struggle, the strong influence of my early training and love for my parents prevailed over the temporary temptation to change my sense of values. I continued to visit the Riggs from time to time, but after that winter I never again lived close enough to Portland to have much contact with them.

A set of circumstances led up to another weekend experience. Indirectly it came about because of a work-relief project for the unemployed, the rebuilding of the highway between Portland and St. Helens. During the winter months the highway was in such a chaotic condition that the Wilark bus, bound for Portland, could not go any farther than St. Helens, so I went the rest of the way by train. On my return trip I rode the train from Portland's Union Station to St. Helens and then took the bus to Wilark.

125

During one of those Sunday evening train rides, a foreman on the road construction project sat down beside me. As we talked, I learned that his name was Lee, his home was on Portland Heights, and that he was a widower with four children. And he was concerned because an elderly, incompetent housekeeper was in charge of them while he was away. When he heard that I was a teacher and not as young as I appeared to be (which he deduced after asking me how long I'd taught), he immediately showed an interest in becoming better acquainted. I wondered if he might have the notion that a teacher—having worked with youngsters—would be more receptive to the idea of being a stepmother. Whatever the reason for his interest, he continued to seek me out whenever I rode on the train and he urged me to come to St. Helens so he could take me to dinner.

> Not only is there the obstacle of being unable to make bus connections, but also the cost ($1.75 round trip fare from Wilark to St. Helens) is no small item. Besides, imagine my leaping down there to meet a man who is only a casual acquaintance. Of course, it may come to that eventually, but I will have to have a drastic change of heart before it does.

One winter day the county health nurse drove out to Wilark on a supposedly routine school visit. Before this she had always been strictly impersonal in her dealings with me, but that afternoon she surprised me by striking up a friendly conversation during which she asked me if I'd ever taught in eastern Oregon. When I replied in the affirmative, she casually mentioned that she knew someone who had helped build the new highway along Summer Lake and she thought it might be interesting for us to meet. Then she went on to explain that this person was now the resident engineer in charge of the road construction between Portland and St. Helens. It seemed that my fellow train passenger had told the engineer about my having once taught at Summer Lake so he wanted to meet me.

> January 25, 1932 .
> Why this great change in Lee is more than I can understand. Heretofore, he has repeatedly asked me to call him if I'm ever in St. Helens, so he can take me out to dinner and a show, and now he

suddenly decides that heaven and earth must be moved to bring his boss and me together.

The resident engineer is forty and divorced so I'm not expecting much from the encounter. Lee and the school nurse have it all planned that the four of us will go out to dinner next Sunday afternoon and then I'll come back out here on the evening bus. But the weather is bad, so I probably won't be able to join them.

January 28, 1932

We think that we (even Esther) shall probably have to stay out here this weekend due to much snow—eighteen inches to two feet on the level. The bus went off the road, so we aren't risking our necks or even taking chances on losing a day's work.

This county road is so narrow and has so many twists and turns as it winds up to the summit of the mountains that it makes a timid passenger turn pale. It is especially dangerous on the narrow curves during the snow. Also the road slants in the wrong direction in some places, so cars slide off the outside edge.

On Wednesday a letter from the school nurse informed me that they all had been disappointed when I had not appeared on Sunday. The revised plan called for the four of us to meet at the bus depot in St. Helens on the following Friday. From there we would go to dinner and afterwards the engineer would take me on to Portland.

February 3, 1932

It would be fun if he were as nice as she says he is, but, oh dear, the handicap of being a forty-year-old Romeo. Maybe he won't like me anyway. Still, I'll have my hair freshly shampooed and be dressed up fit to dazzle my would-be admirer!

February 8, 1932

It's true that my shampoo was a success. At least my escort complimented me on my hair and liked the "Silver Poppies" perfume I was wearing, but that's *all* that was a success.

Just one more instance of a man being too hard

127

for me. It really makes me sick and hopeless-feeling. I thought that this man, being older and having a responsible position (and, therefore, presumably intelligent) might be different. But gosh, it's the same old story. They try you out.

My appearance must deceive men so they think that I'm somewhat sophisticated. Maybe I shouldn't try so hard to look stylish. Even Esther told me one time that I have the air of being self-assured and knowing what it's all about.

The engineer was *nice* and oh, so gorgeously big, with such an air of quiet capability, that for a minute my spirits leaped, and I thought that at last I'd found someone I could fall for. But no. On the way to Portland after dinner he must be like the rest and try to be paid for his company by getting a thrill out of me.

I guess I'm not made for this flirting and love game—maybe my mind has developed at the expense of my emotions. But I rather doubt it. To go back to the old refrain—I wish I could meet someone who is decent and could like him for a change. (When they're too decent, I think they are sissies.) However, it occurs to me that there are other solutions to my problem: (1) I can become less high-minded or (2) grow old as soon as possible.

After Friday night's date was such a fizzle, I was so low in my mind that I was sure that my life would consist exclusively of disappointments, but now I'm determinedly trusting that someone, somewhere, has high enough standards so he will appreciate me for what I am. I'm certainly changing my ideas about the ideal man. It used to be that my qualifications for him included such trivialities as an ability to wear his clothes well, besides a dashing personality, brains, good prospects, etc., but now I'm learning to put likeability, trustworthiness, intelligence, and a regard for another's feelings above everything else. I suppose this means that at last I'm growing up.

I'm beginning to understand what Mama means when she says that a man can have money, position, and a charming personality and still be a miserable failure as a person.

But this is one thing that I am sure of: *Never again will I go on a blind date.*

5

Toward the end of the year I was almost frightened when I thought of the May paycheck being my last one for at least fifteen months. What if I couldn't get a job after I'd earned my degree?

March 11, 1932

I'm not even raising a finger to keep this job, but maybe I should. However, this won't be such a plum next year because Wilark will have a one-room school, and the pay is going to be only $110 a month for the poor teacher who has to teach all eight grades. But that hasn't stopped teachers from wanting the school. Dozens of them have applied for the job.

So, I am definitely committed to a year at the University of Oregon, but the prospect scares me for various reasons. First, there's the financial angle with no income for so long, and second, the thought of being down on the campus competing with all those youngsters. If only I felt more confident, but I'm sure that when I am rested and young-feeling, everything will be fine.

Luckily I was young-looking for my age so I was often asked by people meeting me for the first time if I had just graduated from college. Nevertheless, I continued to have misgivings.

129

April 11, 1932

It won't be long (six weeks) until Wilark will be a part of my past experience. Then what? College—even though it seems unreal in spite of all my scrimping and saving. I can't say that I'm eagerly anticipating the change for I'll be older than the other students, but it may be good for me to be irresponsible again. I don't look any older than a senior co-ed, but coping with characters like Dominick, Sam, Ernest, Earl, and Clifford for the last six years has left some wrinkles on my disposition. So I can't *feel* as young as a college girl. At least not now after a long winter of teaching.

Other times I was full of anticipation.

March 24, 1932

Only eight weeks of school left. Then for a good long vacation away from attendance registers, monthly report cards, and giggling, inattentive pupils.

April 10, 1932

Oh boy—just six more weeks of school.

May 7, 1932

In two weeks I shall have completed my sixth year of teaching which, I must confess, have been good years on the whole. Still, I'm looking forward to a year away from the classroom (where I'm in charge.)

May 13, 1932

A week from today will be the last day of school. After that there should be some big changes in store for Gracie!

Throughout the school year I had been working on the Survey of American Literature correspondence course, and I still had to finish two lessons before summer school opened. Those were probably the dullest and hardest four hours of college credit I ever earned. I decided that even the most boring instructor in class is to be preferred to working alone preparing lessons for an unknown someone who scribbles impersonal comments on the border of one's paper before returning it.

The weekend before our school closed, I dutifully accompanied the eighth graders to their graduation exercises in St. Helens. On the final day of school we had the usual picnic and that evening Mary had us over one more time to dinner—"good dishes, napkins, place cards, and delicious chicken were items." I still have the dainty little card decorated with a ribbon and now faded forgetme-nots which she had by my plate. As I read the original poem which she had written on it, I see that she stressed the thought that one must keep "The old friends with the new/For the old friends are tried and true."

Esther was to be married early in June so she, too, would not be returning to Wilark. We each gathered up and took away the articles that we had earlier enthusiastically contributed to make the shack cozy and homelike. Stripped of the colorful curtains and brightly painted furniture, I wrote that the shack
> looked quite forlorn—all that remained were the
> district's piano, the horrible old rocker that we
> never replaced, and a Congoleum rug on the living
> room floor—thus ended our two-year sojourn at
> Wilark.

UNIVERSITY OF OREGON
1932-1933

When it was time for the 1932 summer school session to open in Portland, I went to stay with a middle-aged couple whom I had met through my sister-in-law.

June 15, 1932

> This session I'm taking some stiff courses—Economics (oh, unhappy thought!), Shakespeare I and Survey of English Literature— no "pipe" courses there for sure.
>
> I've been talking with school authorities who should know, and they say that every course I take from now on must be a required one. It seems that I've been taking too many electives these past few summers so my norms are crying for attention.
>
> My two English classes are taught by Dr. Lesch, a tall, good-looking young professor from an Ivy League college who is reported to be a bachelor. Most of the class members are lady teachers in town from the hinterlands, and they almost drool as they gaze at his broad shoulders so effectively displayed by well-tailored suits.

But not all the class members were under Dr. Lesch's spell. A young man who sat next to me was a full-time student at the University of Oregon, and from his disgusted comments about the coeds on campus who chased after our instructor, I suspected he might be a bit envious.

Unlike previous years, summer school in 1932 did not provide me with an opportunity to meet former classmates from normal school. They were all married by then, and since that automatically barred them from teaching in most districts during the Depression, there was no point in their making the effort to earn a degree. But while I was registering, I had encountered Ruth Melendy, a serious minded and highly intelligent young woman who had been in my class at Franklin High School. Occasionally, we ate lunch together and went to a matinee, but most of the time I walked downtown by myself during the noon hour. On one of these walks I became acquainted with another summer school student.

> One of the students whom I had seen in the halls at school but had never spoken to in my life, adroitly contrived a way to meet me by parking his car across the street and coming over to where I was. He walked beside me for a ways and then began to chat with me about summer school topics. After we'd gone a couple of blocks, he asked me to have lunch with him. I realized that I was being picked up but decided that it might be all right to accept his invitation because we were fellow students. Besides, he wasn't at all "fresh." And he is so wonderfully big that he makes me feel petite.

Neither of us had anything scheduled for that afternoon, so after we had eaten, we went for a ride and I learned quite a bit about the young man. He was approximately my age, had been on the football teams of four different schools, ranging from the University of Oregon to small private colleges, and he still did not have his degree. He acknowledged that his principal aim in life was to have a good time, but he had a delightful personality so I continued to go out with him. A week or so later I wrote:

> It's so much fun whenever we're together because his sense of humor and mine are the same. In that respect he is more of a kindred spirit than anyone I've met since Van Withers of Summer Lake.

I was sure of a fun-filled time, that is, until his "eat, drink, and be merry" philosophy came to the fore and spoiled everything. The Volstead Act was still in effect so I couldn't see myself sneaking into some illegal beer parlor to drink with him, and there were other matters about which we didn't agree, which also disturbed my peace of mind.

> Darn me! Darn these men! And while I'm about it, I might as well darn the world. The awful truth is that I'm out of step in this era of sophistication. Everything's such a *mess*. When one person holds out for what he considers his moral values, another person looks on him as being narrow-minded and prudish.

One day when my landlady, Lulu Belle, and I were discussing what most men seemed to expect on a date, she offered this advice, "Well, Grace, if you can't please them by being yourself, they won't think any more of you if you try to be modern."

That was just about what I would have expected my mother to say under the circumstances, but it carried more weight coming from Lulu Belle because her outlook was more worldly and up-to-date than my mother's. I paid attention to what she said and it helped me to come to some conclusions.

> At the risk of being repetitious, I shall again make a declaration of my point of view. By this time I should have enough respect for myself to remember that there are some people who think I'm a fairly interesting person just the way I am. So from now on I'm not going to let anyone whom I may encounter give me the feeling that I'm the one who is in the wrong. I guess this means that my amusing friend and I have come to a parting of the ways. Too bad that we couldn't have had the same philosophy because he is so much fun.

The next day I was in a better mood:

> I just think I'll have to prove that I do rate and am not such a punk after all. Yesterday one of the Lit class members, who expected to be absent, asked me to find out about her makeup work. Today after class I talked to dashing Dr. Lesch about the matter. When we had finished that bit of conversation, he said, "Miss Brandt, I'm very pleased with your work." As I modestly lowered my eyes,

he went on to compliment me on my knowledge of history which helps me to understand English literature. Then he wanted to know if I had taught and where. When I said, "In a logging camp," he "tsk-tsked" and said that I deserved a better place.

I couldn't resist my old explanation about the pay being generous out there and made it sound more noble by saying that I had been saving to go to college. He was duly impressed by this ambitious young lady standing before him and if we had been alone, *might* have asked me to go to lunch with him. But Ruth was standing there waiting for me, and he had a disciple waiting to talk to him, so we didn't get any further.

Ruth and I lunched together, but she finished first and went on ahead to buy tickets to *The Desert Song.* I was on my way to meet her at the theater when I saw a summer school teacher coming down the street. Since I was feeling well-fed and in a good mood, I smiled at him. He, not knowing me from Cleopatra because I'm not one of his students, looked puzzled but spoke. I went on and as I paused to look for Ruth among the people lined up for tickets, I saw the professor by my side. He had followed me all the way down the block to apologize for the lack of heartiness in his greeting. Then he asked me to have lunch with. He's the absent-minded professor type from Heidelburg—about thirty-five and nice looking. It *would* be my luck to have already eaten and made plans for the afternoon.

July 30, 1932

Not too long before this session of summer school will be over. It seems as if Dr. Lesch has decided that I'm the smart one. This pleases me but is also a strain because one of these days I'm not going to be able to come up with the right

answer when he calls expectantly on me for some
historical background, and then I'll feel
ridiculous.

Probably it was my identification of a Bible verse that first caused him to consider me the "smart one." He had quoted: "Though I
speak with the tongue of men and angels and have not charity, I am
become as a sounding brass or a tinkling cymbal," and then asked
if anyone could give the source. Having listened for years to my
eighth graders recite that verse and the rest of the chapter as one of
the memorizations required by the State Course of Study, I nonchalantly replied, "First Corinthians, Chapter 13, Verse 1."

I never forgot the pleased look of approbation that he then gave
me which rather amused me because almost any eighth grade
teacher in Oregon would have recognized Paul's discourse on
Charity. But naturally the young professor didn't know that, I
didn't bother to enlighten him.

As I despondently pored over the list of courses required for
graduation and saw how many I lacked, I was also forced to consider the fact that some of my normal school credits would not be
accepted by the university. All in all, my prospects for having a
degree by the following June were not good, so I stopped after class
one day to seek Dr. Lesch's advice. I asked him if it might be possible for me to take a correspondence course in the interval between summer school and fall term in order to pick up some extra
credits. Of course, he could not give me a definite answer until he
knew more about the situation, so he suggested that we meet the
following day to study my college transcript. After that meeting,
Dr. Lesch made arrangements for me to take Shakespeare II as a
correspondence course after the close of summer session with him
as my instructor. At the same time he promised to take me to the
head of the history department when I arrived on campus, and between the two of them they would devise a way for me to squeeze
in all my requirements.

All this time my studies and extra-curricular activities had occupied much of my attention, but when I returned to the farm after

summer school, I was jolted to discover that the Depression was growing ever deeper.

All summer I've been hearing people gloomily predicting that there will be a slow uphill grade to recovery which has made me wonder about the wisdom of my plans for next winter.

To make matters worse close to home, the folks have been unable to sell their berry crop so their income for the year will be practically nothing—just like everyone else around here who raises berries for a living. Of course, they're no worse off than other farmers because all farm produce is terribly low—lettuce sells at five heads for a nickel, prunes 15 cents for a bushel. And hamburger is ten cents a pound in the butcher shop, so the cattle grower must not be getting much.

If I had known in the spring that berries were going to be such a flop, I would have forgotten about college, but now I am committed. I gave up my job, and this late in the summer I couldn't get another one for love or money.

When I worry, it is that remarkable mother of mine who cheers me up by staunchly insisting that I'm doing the right thing. I know her firm support is based upon a concern for my health (I've had lots of colds that hang on and on) and the conviction that I need a rest from the strain of the classroom and troublesome pupils.

My college fund was directly affected by the price of berries because I had loaned $100 to my older sister's husband during the winter. When he had asked me for the money, it was understood that I would be repaid after he harvested his berry crop, but now that was impossible. And my brother was finding it impossible to pay back the money I'd loaned to him in 1928.

Later in the summer I learned that the savings and loan company where I had so confidently deposited my money at a higher rate of interest was now bankrupt. My plans to withdraw the eighty dollars I had invested there never materialized because I was letting it draw interest until the last minute before I left for college. I gratefully remembered that the rest of my savings were in a postal savings account that was safe as long as the United States government remained stable.

One other bright spot in the gloom was the arrival of a letter from Mr. Rees, Stanfield's school clerk announcing that the warrants I was holding were finally being called in. Now $250 plus thirty dollars in interest could be added to my postal savings funds.

The correspondence course with Dr. Lesch was to be completed by September fifteenth so I started working on it as soon as I received the assignments. When I became too weary of Shakespeare, I left my books and went for a ride on Sparkie, the pony that had joined Lady and Nig on the farm after my younger sister heard that he was half-starved and in need of a good home. After I donated the fifteen dollars to buy him, Clarice took over. She fed and groomed him until he looked like the fine riding horse he really was. It was a joy to ride Sparkie because of his smooth and easy gait, so when he took me for long jaunts over the countryside, I was sure that the fifteen dollars was a sum well spent.

Clarice Brandt riding Sparkie, the spirited riding horse that Grace bought for $15 in 1932. On the family farm near Boring, Oregon.

After I finished the course and received my grade, I appreciatively wrote:

> Dr. Lesch, the sweet personality, sent me my grade without subjecting me to an exam—and what a grade—"A!" I was really proud although I'm afraid I don't deserve it (she says modestly.)

He included a little note expressing the hope that I'd look him up when I "came down" to the campus.

One week before I left for Eugene, I withdrew $100.00 from my postal savings account and deposited the money in the bank where I had a checking account. I then wrote a check for twenty dollars which was to be used for Sparkie's winter feed and gave it to my mother. On that same day she and my father hurried to exchange it for hay and grain. I, however, carefully refrained from writing any more checks because I wanted to have at least eighty dollars in my account to meet registration and other first-week-of-school expenses.

The summer had been a busy one, so there had been no time to worry about my future role as a student on the University of Oregon campus. But when I could actually count the hours until I left home for college. I began to have some qualms.

> I wish I were going down to Eugene with a friend so I wouldn't have the feeling that I am going to be a stranger in a foreign land. I know that I'll become acquainted as soon as classes start, and even before that I'll have roommates at the Dorm. (I do hope that fate doesn't put me in with some eighteen-year old.)
>
> Sometimes I wish I could be in a sorority but that is merely snobbishness on my part. I suppose that the only reason I want to belong is because not everyone can, and it would please my ego to be one of the chosen few—.
>
> "But, Grace! You're supposed to be going down there to *study*." (Mama's refrain.)
>
> And of course she's absolutely right.

2

I arrived at the University on Tuesday forenoon. I located my room at the dormitory, ate lunch, and then went to see Dr. Lesch. After we had exchanged greetings, I told him that I was hoping he'd not forgotten his promise to help me with my schedule. He assured me that he hadn't and went to the phone to call Dr. Clarke, head of the history department, to ask for an appointment.

I was somewhat surprised when I saw Dr. Clarke the next day. Instead of the precise, dry, scholarly type that I had envisioned him to be, the professor was relaxed and unassuming in dress and manner. In fact, he could have been mistaken for a kindly country doctor.

Later, after he and Dr. Lesch had spent hours painstakingly outlining my classwork for the year, it was apparent that I would have to carry eighteen hours every term in order to graduate in June. Then as they planned my fall term schedule, they found it impossible to avoid conflicts. Dr. Clarke solved this problem by setting up a special reading and conference course for which he would be my instructor.

The good professors' efforts on my behalf had two beneficial results: I knew exactly which classes I should take in order to fulfill the requirements for a degree, and as I left Dr. Clarke's office, I knew that I was not entirely friendless in this new setting.

It was freshman and transfer-student week on campus so the dormitory was almost empty except for a few students. It was also Rush Week for the sororities so I could hear a bustle of activity in a few of the other rooms on my floor at certain hours, especially late in the afternoon just before the dinner hour. Then there was silence after the rooms' occupants hurried away to be entertained by a sorority. Silence, except for a phone down the hall which rang incessantly but was never answered. Finally, late in the afternoon on Thursday someone answered it and I heard her shout, "Is there anybody on this floor named Grace Brandt?"

I rushed to the door, opened it, and called back, "Yes, there is. *I'm* Grace Brandt!"

"Well, you're wanted on the phone."

It was a call from the Kappa Delta sorority inviting me to dinner that evening. The girl on the other end of the line apologized for giving me such brief notice and explained that after calling me all week this was the first time the sorority had been able to contact me. I accepted the invitation and memorized the address she gave me.

Now that I was in friendly communication with the rest of the world again, I was pleased and excited. A chance to see the inside of a sorority house! I chose a dress with the greatest of care, and after that decision was made spent the next hour and half making ready for the thrilling occasion. When I was satisfied that I had done all I could to enhance my appearance, I started out.

I found the correct address and was effusively greeted by girls formally dressed for dinner. It was Rush Week so all the Chapter members exuded charm. Whatever feelings of rejection I might have had during the week were forgotten the instant I stepped across the sorority's threshold. Everyone I met hung on my words and laughed appreciatively at my attempts to be humorous. Someone complimented me on my dress, and later another girl was enthusiastic about the cameo ring I was wearing. Several times in answer to an interested inquiry I disclosed my major subject and told something about my teaching experiences. In fact, my listeners seemed to be fascinated by everything I had ever done or expected to do. It was wonderful to be the center of so much attention. I was convinced that never before had I been in such good company.

After I was back at the dormitory that night, I began to wonder how the sorority knew of my presence on the campus. Then I remembered hearing Sylvia recall with pride her days as a sorority girl when she was a student at Oregon Agriculture College in Corvallis and I had a vague recollection of hearing her sing the praises of Kappa Delta. So I came to the conclusion that it was Sylvia who was responsible for calling me to the attention of the chapter on the University of Oregon campus.

Except for what I'd heard from Sylvia, I knew very little about Greek letter organizations, but her enthusiasm had led me to think

141

of them as something very special, and belonging to one, a privilege which left its mark on one's life forevermore. Especially so if one were fortunate enough to be a Kappa Delta as she was. Therefore, I was inclined to like the idea of accepting the sorority's bid in spite of the extra money it would cost me.

To make sure that I was acting wisely, though, I went to the Dean of Women for advice. After I had filled her in with most of the details, she asked me if I'd ever lived in a dormitory before. When I said that I had lived in one at Oregon Normal School, that seemed to simplify the matter for her.

"In that case," she said, "sorority life could be a broadening experience, a way of life completely new to you. From that aspect alone it should be worth the extra money it costs to live in a sorority. And as for your being too old for that sort of thing, I don't think you'll find the age gap more noticeable there than in the dorm."

Since the Dean had pointed out that sorority life could be considered an experience, a further enrichment to be derived from my year at the university, it put the question in a different light. If I joined, it need not necessarily be for purely snobbish reasons.

Later when I was invited to join, I agreed to become a Kappa Delta pledge.

The other pledges to Kappa Delta that year were three freshman girls who also had been staying in the dormitory. Since it was customary for the future roommates of the pledges to help them move into the chapter house, four girls from the sorority arrived at the dorm Saturday afternoon with a truck and driver.

I was pleased to see that Virginia Wentz, a senior, would be my roommate because I had enjoyed her good-natured humor when we were dinner partners at the chapter house the two previous evenings. It was no great chore for Virginia, better known as "Ginny," to help me move because all the belongings I had brought from home were in a wardrobe trunk and one suitcase. The driver loaded all the trunks and then climbed back into the truck to wait until the rest of the girls' possessions were brought out to the curb. Ginny and I had plenty of time to wait before that was accomplished, so we stood to one side observing the others work. Apparently it didn't occur to either that we might offer our help.

My attention was caught by Maxine Rau, an "active" Kappa Delta, and Helen Taylor, the pledge who was to be Maxine's roommate. In addition to numerous pieces of luggage, Helen had an unbelievably large collection of boxes which contained pictures, pennants, fancy sofa pillows, and stuffed animals. I saw Maxine go to the elevator for the heavy suitcases that had just been brought down from Helen's dormitory room and after she lugged those to the truck, she attacked the pile of boxes.

All this time I was struck by the change in her attitude. At the dinner parties she had been the embodiment of gracious charm. But that was during Rush Week which was now in the past. Helen had committed herself to the sorority so there was no further need for Maxine to go out of her way to be pleasant to her. Anyone could see that she disliked this moving job and I suspected that she didn't care who knew it.

After we pledges were moved into the chapter house, I discovered that Maxine's behavior was typical of all the girls. They were exhausted by their efforts to get new members—sick of smiling and having to pretend interest. From now on we pledges were on our own and would be accepted or merely tolerated according to our merits.

On Wednesday of my second week at the university I received a phone call from the registrar's office. A woman's voice sympathetically informed me that the checks I had written for registration fees had been returned with the notice that the bank upon which they were drawn was now closed. Later I learned that it closed its doors less than a week after I deposited the $100, so every check that I had written the first ten days of school had to be replaced. All there was to show for the money I had withdrawn from Postal Savings while I was home was twenty dollars worth of horse feed. There wouldn't have been even that if my parents hadn't rushed to cash my check as soon as I gave it to them. My college fund was growing smaller and smaller but I hoped that I still had enough to see me through the school year.

My roommate, Ginny, and Maxine were close friends so Maxine spent most of her spare time in our room. What I remember best are the many evenings when they studied their French lessons together. As they conjugated verbs, they laughed and joked and were highly amused by their mistakes in translating. It sounded like fun—nobody liked a joke better than I—but I was carrying eighteen hours instead of the customary sixteen, so I would forfeit the extra two hours if I received any grade less than a "B." And in those days a student needed to do super-superior work to receive a "B" because grading was done on the percentage curve. This meant that the instructors were expected to grade the majority of the students a "C," a much smaller percent of the class enrollment a "B," and even fewer earned the "As." I did wish Ginny and Maxine wouldn't make such a lark out of their study sessions.

By late October I saw that the thirty-five dollar board bill plus monthly sorority fees were more than I could afford, so I began to think about moving out of the chapter house for that reason, and also because it was proving to be a noisy place for studying. From past experience I knew that batching was a sure way to lower living expenses so I was interested when three young women invited me to share their housekeeping rooms in a private home.

One of them, Cecelia Brennan, was in two of my history classes so it was through her that I had met the other two girls, Louise Howard and Mildred Widmer. They all were near my age, and like me, had earned money for this year at the university by teaching school. Their invitation was too good an opportunity to pass by so I deposited five dollars (my monthly share of the rent) with the landlady and made plans to move in with them the following Saturday.

When I casually mentioned my intentions at the sorority house, I was astounded by the agitation it caused among the members. Dorothy MacLean, who had a dynamic personality, was president of Kappa Delta. She assumed control in what they all seemed to consider a crisis by taking me aside to hear my reasons for wanting to move.

I first mentioned that I needed a quieter place to study and hurried on to say, "Now, don't misunderstand me. It isn't that I don't like Ginny. No one could help liking a person who is as full of fun as she is, but that's the trouble. She attracts so many people to our room that there's never a quiet moment when she's around."

Dort nodded and shrugged her shoulders. "I can believe that," she conceded.

As president, Dorothy rated one of the most attractive and spacious rooms in the house, so it was an inducement to stay when she said, "I don't have a roommate, so how would you like to move in with me? My room is off by itself. It's quieter back there, and most of the time it's empty because I go to the smoking room where I can smoke and study at the same time."

The smoking room was the only place in the sorority where smoking was allowed. This was true of all the living organizations for women on the campus and in accordance with university regulations.

I appreciated her offer because it meant sacrificing the privacy which I knew she valued, but there was still the question of money, so I replied, "That's awfully good of you, Dort. I know I'd love that room, but I might as well admit that I just can't afford to pay what it's costing me to live here—the fees, and all. If I batch, it'll be a whole lot cheaper than the thirty-five dollars I pay here. Probably something like twenty dollars or lower."

Dort thought a minute. "We'll cut your board and room to twenty-five dollars and forget the house dues."

This was a generous concession, one that could make a big difference in my expenditures for the year. And then I suddenly realized that the *real* reason for my wanting to move was that I did not like sorority life. I wanted to be with people my age whose experience was similar to mine. But I could hardly admit that to Dort so I brought forth my last point with complete confidence that it was a clincher.

"That would make a big difference, all right. But I'm afraid it's too late. I've already paid five dollars in rent money to the woman who owns the apartment, and judging by her appearance, I don't think there's a chance in the world that she'd let go of it."

To that, Dort immediately came back with, "If I can get her to give it up, will you stay here?"

I felt perfectly safe in agreeing to Dort's terms because I couldn't imagine any landlady during the Depression voluntarily relinquishing a down payment that rightfully belonged to her. How astonished I was the next day when Dort triumphantly returned the rent money to me! I've often wondered what she could have said that would cause the woman to refund that five dollars.

145

It was not until I was an "active member" (after I had been initiated) that I learned why there had been so much concern when I announced that I was leaving. Like so many other anxieties in those days, it could be traced back to an inadequate income. The Kappa Delta sorority enjoyed a high rating nationally, but this local chapter was a fairly new one so it had not had time to become a strong organization before the Depression hit. After that, fewer girls could afford to go to college and even fewer to join a sorority. Those who did affiliated with the largest, most prestigious, house on campus from which they received a bid. Kappa Delta at the University of Oregon was neither large nor prestigious. Therefore, it was difficult for it to attract the number of good-caliber girls needed to meet the costs of maintaining the chapter house and paying off its mortgage. Every member's contribution was desperately needed. All of which explains why my sorority sisters were so anxious to keep me in their midst even if I paid less than the usual amount.

After Dort's truly heroic encounter with the landlady, there could be no question about my remaining at the sorority house so I moved into her room. It had a southern exposure and I have pleasant memories of coming back from classes to study in the quiet, sun-filled room.

After I received my midterm examination grades, I knew that I need not feel anxious about my ability to earn all B's or better. I relaxed and took time to look around me.

"These, for better or for worse, are my sorority sisters," I thought, "so I might just as well learn to like them and enter into the spirit of this learning experience that the Dean of Women recommended so highly."

3

Some of the girls were almost fanatically loyal to Kappa Delta and constantly sought ways to add to its glory. Early in the fall I was inveigled into one of these efforts when they needed someone to represent our house in an inter-sorority swim meet. I had once made the mistake of mentioning that I could swim pretty well even though I was not as athletic as some of the other members of the sorority. I hadn't meant to imply that I was an expert swimmer because goodness knows, I was aware of my limitations. I had never had a swimming lesson in my life. As a child I accidently learned to swim while playing in a creek with another little girl. My water-wings fell off, and it was either sink or swim so I dog-paddled to the nearest log, and thereafter I considered myself a swimmer. As I grew older, I swam in any body of water around Portland that was available—rivers, creeks, lakes, or public swimming pools—and became comparatively fast in the water but not good enough to be in competition.

I told the girls so when they wanted me to be in the meet, but they wouldn't listen to me then, nor when I protested that I shouldn't even get my feet wet because I was almost sick with a cold. Every argument was brushed aside as inconsequential compared with the possibility that I might win some recognition for Kappa Delta. They implied that I was being a traitor to our group so I finally quit resisting and agreed to go. Three of the more insistent girls who were free that hour accompanied me to the gymnasium. As we walked along I had the feeling that I was being offered as a sacrifice on the altar of Kappa Delta.

When we arrived and I saw the husky, self-confident physical education majors standing on the edge of the pool, I knew that the result would be the same as if I had stayed back at the chapter house, but I also knew that the presence of my sorority sisters doomed me to go through the motions of competing.

On the first lap I did quite well until I came to the end of the lane and had to turn around for the second lap. Then I was outclassed. My competitors had been taught the tricks of the trade so they were turned around and six feet ahead of me before I managed to get myself turned and headed in the right direction. The more laps we swam, the farther behind I was.

As I walked home with my dejected companions, I was almost glad that I'd made as poor a showing as I had said I would. Maybe they'd pay more attention to me next time, I thought. And when my cold worsened so I had to miss classes for two days, I had to remind myself quite often to be charitable, to remember that even though my sorority sisters were overzealous sometimes, they really hadn't intended that I should be threatened with pneumonia.

During the winter a few of the upperclassmen decided that, in addition to being concerned about getting public recognition for the sorority, there should also be consideration for the quality of life within the chapter house. They proposed to help members rid themselves of annoying habits by having a "Truth Session" which was a popular fad on the campus that winter. One evening we gathered together and spent the next couple of hours pointing out each other's irritating ways. Since almost everyone tried to remember that the session's purpose was to make us live together more harmoniously, there were't *too* many brutally frank comments.

When I was found blameworthy for my sharp wit, I wasn't entirely surprised because I was aware that sometimes my humorous comments were too pointed for comfort. All these years I have remembered that criticism, so ultimately it may have helped me to change for the better. At the time, however, I did not feel particularly chastened—probably because my accuser was finding fault with so many of us.

It hurt, though, when someone else commented that my English brogues made too much noise when I walked on the bare hardwood floors of the chapter house. Those expensive imported oxfords were my pride and joy, and when I wore them it was the fulfillment of a longing that went back to my days at normal school where I had envied the girls who wore the thick-soled shoes which I couldn't afford to buy. Later when I had the money to buy them, there was no reason to because they were too noisy for everyday wear in the schoolroom. But brogues were still in style on the college campuses in 1932 so naturally I purchased the sturdiest, heaviest-soled pair I could find and immediately had steel plates put on the heels. As I walked around the campus in them, it gave me confidence to know that in one respect at least I was convincingly collegiate. Now during this "Truth Session" my shoes were being criticized.

"I certainly don't have money to buy another pair," I thought indignantly. "There's not much I can do about the noise—unless they expect me to walk around the house in my stocking feet."

However, on second thought I had to admit that there was room for improvement so after that I trod more softly. This made it quieter for the others, but the criticism had taken something out of my life. Never again did I have the same sense of pride when I wore my expensive brogues.

After fall midterm exams I had firmly resolved to enjoy life in the sorority house, but when it came to the house duties assigned to me as a pledge, I wavered. The one I disliked most was scrubbing out our housemother's bathtub. It seemed just too demeaning, somehow, and I couldn't help wondering why she didn't do it for herself, but I realized that there were many things I didn't understand about sororities.

When it was my turn to vacuum and dust the living room and its adjoining music room alcove, I liked that duty because everyone could see and appreciate the results of my labor. Finally I volunteered to assume full responsibility for keeping those two rooms cleaned in exchange for being relieved of all other pledge duties. The house manager was only too glad to accept my offer. She had seen what the rooms looked like during the weeks when the young pledges gave them a once-over-lightly treatment.

Every detail of managing the local chapter was in the hands of the members because our housemother had no responsibilities beyond those serving as our hostess and chaperone. She was not one of those housemothers who are friends and confidants to the girls in their sororities because her aloof manner discouraged any thought we might have had of going to her for advice or encouragement. She was a small, elegant-looking, brown-eyed woman with prematurely white hair who presided graciously at all of our social functions. Of course, she was an authority on etiquette—as all housemothers had to be—so from observing her closely I learned how to properly open a baked potato at the dinner table. I've always thought that this was a concrete example of the cultural enrichment that the Dean of Women promised would be mine if I joined a sorority.

Our sorority was not one of the socially prominent ones at the University, but it did occasionally entertain with a tea or a dessert dance, which didn't cost much, and once a term there was a formal dance. Getting ready for any social function called for more than the usual amount of time and effort because we did not own many of the articles that are needed to make a good impression on guests. Therefore, we had to borrow them from the families of our active members or alumni who lived in Eugene.

When we were preparing for the winter term formal dance, I was one of the members appointed to go pick up a punch bowl set, candelabra, and sundry other decorative dishes that were borrowed ever so often from an alum's generous mother. It was a never-to-be-forgotten experience because the alum's father held the mortgage on our chapter house. As his wife and daughter hurried around filling a box with fine crystal and sterling silver articles, he bitterly aired his grievances which had to do with the delinquency of our mortgage payments.

Giving in to his daughter's coaxing several years before, he had made this investment which was proving to be a disaster. And he wasn't letting his wife, daughter, or anyone connected with Kappa Delta—including us—forget it. After properly thanking the kind mother for her generosity, we hurriedly left the premises. On the way home we unanimously agreed to let someone else return the articles and have the experience of facing the unhappy man who held our mortgage.

I don't remember whether I enjoyed the fruits of my labor by attending the dance that night, but I am certain that I went to at least one of our formal dances because I recall wearing the black formal dress that I'd bought for such occasions. I have no idea who my partner was or where I found him.

If I had gone down to the University hopefully expecting to be a part of its social life, I would have been woefully disappointed. When my sorority invited fraternities in for a dessert dance, the young men who showed up were too young for me chronologically and lacked experience in the work-a-day world.

150

One day I went to the Anchorage with my sorority sisters for a coke. The Anchorage was the gathering place for the "beautiful people" on campus, the Betty Coed and Joe College types. While we were there, a group of fraternity men entered the place and sauntered self-confidently past the row of booths where groups of sorority girls were sitting. One of them chanted out the name of the sorority each group belonged to as he came to it. "Chi O's," "Kappas," "Thetas," "Tri Delts," "A O Pi's," etc., and when he came to us, "Kay Dees."

It made me think of us as being members of different castes and I resented it. Besides that, I felt infinitely older and more experienced than the self-assured young people in there enjoying their sheltered little world. I felt old but unfortunately, I was not old enough or mature enough to be objective about the students and their meeting place.

And later when Dr. Lesch invited me to go to the Anchorage with him, I discovered that I was not so poised after all. I shrank from the prospect of walking into the students' midst with the popular Dr. Lesch and being subjected to their stares. The very fact that he evidently liked the place made me wonder if we had much in common, so I gave him some obviously feeble excuse for not going. My instructor philosophized in class the next day about people who stifled their emotions and were afraid to show their feelings.

4

Being a student was my occupation that year so what went on off campus seemed to be far, far away. But I was interested when Franklin Delano Roosevelt won the presidential election in November, 1932, and later I read the news items and editorials about his March 4, 1933, inaugural address in which he made the famous statement, "First of all, let me assert my firm belief that the only thing we have to fear is fear itself—nameless unreasoning, unjustified terror which paralyzes needed efforts to convert retreat into advance."

At last, here was something uplifting to think about after years of hearing nothing but gloom!

Later, on March 12, I heard him give his first "fireside chat." I was a guest in the home of Mr. and Mrs. Douglas whom I met on the Alaskan cruise in 1930. Mr. Douglas was head of the university library, so I had looked them up when I entered college that fall. They made me feel welcome in their home, and that Sunday had invited me and two faculty members for dinner which was scheduled early enough so we could listen to the widely-publicized fireside chat.

When the president was through talking to us ("Friends, my fellow Americans") in that beautifully modulated voice of his, I felt a first, faint stirring of hope that the Depression would eventually come to an end.

It was good to be able to hope that the country's economy was on its way to recovery, but as I looked for a teaching position that spring I saw no evidence of a change for the better. I haunted the university's employment bureau but the people there were of little help because they seldom heard from a district in need of a teacher. Anyone who had a teaching position was holding on to it. Finally the bureau notified me that a teacher was needed at Cascade Summit on Odell Lake in the heart of the Cascade Mountains. A school board member from there came to the university to interview me and one other applicant, a young man just graduating from college. The board member told us that Cascade Summit was a settlement built by the railroad company for its maintenance crews and their families. Being snowbound was an ordinary occurrence during the winter because snow accumulated to a depth of twenty feet or more. He inadvertantly disclosed that this was hard on people's tempers, resulting in neighborhood quarrels—especially among the women. The people in the community wanted a teacher who could teach their one-room school and also give private music lessons. That last requirement eliminated me, but as I was leaving I heard the interviewer interestedly talking to the other applicant who had said he could play a French horn.

Back at the sorority house I thought about the deep snow in that isolated little hamlet in the mountains and felt less disappointed about losing out to the young French horn player. Later though, it became apparent that it was to be the only opening I would hear of for the rest of the school year. Then I began to wonder if being cooped up with a bunch of quarrelsome women wasn't a modest price to pay in exchange for the security of a monthly paycheck.

During final examination week in June my sister Clarice, who had just graduated from high school, came down to spend the end of the school year with me. It was a drolly-humorous experience for both of us because we looked so much alike that people often mistook her for me. She was amused but also embarrassed to be

June, 1933. Grace wearing cap and gown for her University of Oregon graduation picture.

stopped on the campus and asked by more than one person what she thought of a certain test question, etc., or to have a Kappa Delta town girl visiting at the Chapter house talk to her for fifteen minutes and then suddenly say, "Somehow you don't look the same as usual, Grace. Don't you feel well?"

When it came time to attend the baccalaureate and commencement exercises, I was spared the two dollar cost of renting a cap and gown because Mrs. Douglas loaned hers to me. She made a practice of doing this when there was a girl graduate in whom she was especially interested. It was a final evidence of the friendship that she and her husband had shown me throughout the year.

I appreciated the use of the cap and gown for more than sentimental reasons because by then I was having to practice stringent economy. My college fund had shrunk to fifty dollars and, for the first time since I started to teach, there was no prospect for a future income.

5

My return home as a college graduate was not the triumphant experience I had always thought it would be. Although no one ever actually said so, there must have been many people who felt that I had been foolish to give up a well paid position so I could go to college. I do recall hearing one of my married friends say this much, however. "Now *you'll* know what it is like to be out of work," which was rather revealing, I thought.

Since the university's employment bureau continued to be unable to send me the names of places in Oregon where I might apply for a school, I decided to join a commercial teachers' employment agency which had contacts all over the western states. It provided me with the names of communities in remote parts of Colorado, Wyoming, and Montana where a teacher was needed for their one-room schools. I eagerly sent out letters of application but received no response, so I concluded that the school boards in those districts were not impressed by my six years of teaching experience and brand new Bachelor of Science degree in history.

All summer I stayed close to home except for an occasional overnight stay with some of my friends. During the month of July I picked blackcaps and raspberries for my folks but earned only thirteen dollars because I was not an especially fast picker and the going wage was less than a cent per pound.

Ever since childhood the sound of crickets had reminded me that summer was almost gone and school would soon begin. When I first heard them in the summer of 1933, they seemed to be telling me over and over that I still had no school to go to and not much time to find one. By the last week in August I was still among the unemployed, but—just like in a suspense movie—on August 31st I received a call from the Crook County Superintendent of Schools. It was a long distance call but he managed to let me know that if I wanted it, he had a school for me to teach at Paulina in central Oregon. I had never heard of the place, but he made it sould like quite a settlement as he mentioned the hotel, store, one-room school, several residences and community hall to be found there. School was in session for only eight months but I would be paid at the rate of fifty dollars per month for twelve months (six hundred dollars annual salary.)

The superintendent wanted to know before he concluded the call whether or not I would take the school. There was never any question about my accepting the contract after so many months of waiting, but as I hung up the receiver, I was sick at heart. After all that struggle to get a degree, I was doomed to be back in a one-room school, teaching at less than half the salary I had earned at Wilark. I went outdoors to lean against the house and weep tears of bitter disappointment. My father found me there and said, "Why, Gracie! Here you are crying and I would have thought it was a time for rejoicing."

I thought, "He just doesn't understand how much it hurts my pride to be back teaching in a one-room school again. I'm no better off than when I started out at Summer Lake seven years ago."

In a little while, though, I came to my senses and realized how grateful I should be. To show how fully I had recovered, I hurried to town to shop with the thirteen dollars that I'd earned in the berry fields. It was discouraging to discover that it took all of that amount to buy a pair of good-fitting dress shoes, but I bought them anyway.

"Who knows," I thought hopefully, "there might be enough social life in Paulina so I'll really need them."

PAULINA
1933-1934

After I agreed during our phone call to go to Paulina, the superintendent informed me that I was to attend an all-day meeting in Prineville on the following Saturday. That gave me two days to get ready before leaving on Friday morning.

When the bus from Portland arrived in Prineville late Friday afternoon, I climbed out and walked over to the Ochoco Inn which was built of stone with a Spanish motif. It seemed to me that it looked rather out of place among the less pretentious store buildings in that little cattle town with its dusty, unpaved streets. However, when I entered the lobby, I found the Inn lived up to its promise for its interior was equal to that seen in first-rate hotels in much larger towns.

All day Saturday I sat in the sweltering high school gymnasium listening to instructions and inspiring talks, for this meeting was in lieu of a Teachers' Institute. If we weren't actually in session, I asked questions, trying to learn what I could about this part of central Oregon. When I heard that all but two schools in Crook County were of the one-room variety, I knew for sure that I had come to Oregon's wide-open spaces.

Prineville was the only town in Crook County and the site of the county's one high school. When I asked how the youngsters in outlying districts could get a high school education, I was told that they either lived with a town family and paid for their keep, or worked in exchange for their board and room. Prosperous ranchers maintained a residence in Prineville as long as their children were in high school, and in that case the mother lived in town with the youngsters while her husband remained on the ranch.

At the end of the session I met a young woman whom I had noticed at the meetings that day. She stopped and asked if I had a place to board, and mentioned that she lived on a ranch near Paulina, but not in my district. As I told her that Martin Baker, the superintendent, had found a place for me to stay, I thought how kind it was of her to be interested in a total stranger's welfare.

Mr. Baker had also arranged a ride for me with some townspeople who were taking their daughter to her first teaching position at Suplee, thirty miles beyond Paulina. When they came by the hotel to pick me up the next afternoon, I climbed into the car's back seat with my suitcase in hand. There was scarcely room for me and the daughter and her boxes of groceries and furnishings she was taking to the teacherage where she would batch. However, the ride was free so I had no cause for complaint.

Soon the car passed the last signs of habitation in the vicinity of Prineville. Several miles farther on we came to a high point overlooking the surrounding country with a view of a mountain range off in the distance. The girl's father pointed to it with the remark that Paulina and Suplee were in that general direction. Much of the time there was nothing more interesting to see than sagebrush, juniper trees and rimrocks on each side of the road, but occasionally we passed by a ranch in a broad irrigated valley, only to continue on for miles through what appeared to me to be a worthless, sagebrush-covered terrain, but which in reality could be used for grazing.

After a two hour, sixty mile ride over rough and dusty roads, I was told that we would soon be in Paulina. The road at that point was close to the foot of a steep hillside which was to our left. On the opposite side the land gradually sloped toward a level lowland, part of which was irrigated. As we rounded a curve by the schoolhouse, Paulina came into view in the immediate foreground.

My first reaction was one of disappointment because Paulina certainly was not the populous settlement that Mr. Baker's description over the phone had led me to believe it was. It's true it did have a store, a large hall which presumably was the Grange hall he had mentioned, and the driver of the car informed me that the two-story dwelling nearby served as a hotel. But there were only seven unpainted houses scattered around in fenced-off plots of sagebrush and some of them were mere dilapidated shacks. Actually Paulina was nothing but a tiny hamlet. But I had learned from my first teaching experience that news concerning the school teacher is widely circulated in a sparsely settled region, so I gave my companions no intimation of my feelings.

After I learned that it was the largest settlement for sixty miles in any direction, I could understand why Mr. Baker had described it so glowingly. Compared to other isolated communities to be found in Crook County, Paulina was a thriving center of population.

We rode past the hotel, the Grange hall, and came to a well kept store building painted white, with a high porch at the front and a hitching post close by. Here the road turned abruptly to follow for a stone's throw the fence line until it reached a sharp corner where a square, two-story unpainted ranch house stood.

Although our driver lived in Prineville, he had demonstrated ever since we started out that he was amazingly well acquainted with the ranches along the way and their inhabitants. This was again apparent when he stopped the car in front of the ranch house and said, "I guess this is where you get out, Miss Brandt. The Grays live here and, according to Mr. Baker, that's who you are going to live with."

After I dug around and found my suitcase, I got out of the car, thanked the people for my ride, and turned to where my landlady was waiting for me only a few steps away in the doorway. She took me into the dining room to meet her husband and fifteen-year-old son who observed me closely as they tried to decide what kind of a person they had taken into their home. I too was gathering some first impressions. Ola Gray was an attractive, wholesome looking woman in her early thirties who was friendly in a reserved way. On the other hand, her husband, who appeared to be several years older, met me with an open and friendly grin. Their son Billy, who would soon leave home to go to a high school in Clatsop County where he would stay with friends, looked on but didn't have much to say.

Of course, I did not become well acquainted with Ola and Fred Gray that first afternoon, but I knew immediately that they were not unschooled backwoods people who considered anyone from western Oregon an alien. It was a relief to find this first impression of them a favorable one. After we'd talked a while, Ola offered to show me my room. We left the dining room, where we had been sitting, and went into the central hall that extended from the front door to the back of the house. Out in the hall we walked past the stairway leading to the second floor and went into the parlor. It was a well furnished room with a carpet on the floor, rayon drapes at the windows, a heater, and an overstuffed davenport and chair set. At the back, doors led into two small bedrooms, one of which was to be mine. When I entered it, I saw a comfortable looking twin bed with matching dresser and a makeshift closet in one corner.

As we crossed the hall to go back to the other part of the house, Ola told me that until just recently there had been no stove in the parlor because they preferred to use the dining room as a living room. But now they had installed a parlor stove because they thought that it would be nice for the school ma'am to have a place to entertain her beaux. Upon hearing the word "beaux," I perked up. Perhaps—just possibly—this coming year might prove to be an interesting one.

2

The next day was Labor Day so I had an opportunity to inspect the school premises before school opened. I walked a quarter of a mile down the road and crossed over a cattle guard into the fenced-off school yard which had been partly cleared of sagebrush. I saw no playground equipment as I walked across the grounds to the schoolhouse, but I did see a pump and a flagpole. After climbing the steep steps to the unroofed front porch (now we would call it a "deck"), I unlocked the door and entered a cloakroom and from there went on into the classroom. The building was divided into two large classrooms with a folding door separating the schoolroom from the one that was now a catch-all for broken desks, an organ without a keyboard, and sundry other worthless articles.

In one of the back corners of the schoolroom there was a large sheet iron stove with the usual three-foot-high metal shield standing out from it on three sides. Whenever I saw such a shield on a classroom stove, I presumed it was there to catch and circulate the heat so it would not go only to those sitting close by. Whatever its intended function, it was also a safety device which could keep pupils from stumbling into the stove's red hot sides.

Continuing to look around, I saw two windows at the back of the room and twice that many facing the nearby road. There was a limited amount of blackboard space and the minimum of school supplies. When I compared what I saw before me with what I'd had at Wilark, it was disheartening.

The worn board floors were covered with a thick layer of dust because the building had not been used since the last of April. I found the broom and gave the place a good sweeping, deciding as I did so to apply a coat of the floor oil I had seen among the supplies, but that would have to wait until later.

As I walked down the steps to leave, I noticed stacks of pine firewood in back of the building. From a distance it looked easy to chop, which was of no little interest to me for I would be doing the janitor work that year.

On Tuesday morning I reached school early but it wasn't long until the ten pupils who lived in or near Paulina arrived. These were four Gardner children (three boys, one girl) whose family ran the hotel, three children from the Roundtree home which was across the road from my boarding place, Johnzie Faulkner, Betty Miller, and one other girl who was boarding in the community. All the children looked neat and clean in their mail order catalog clothes. The hotel youngsters dominated the conversation with accounts of their immediate family's activities and stories about their grandma, uncles, aunts, and a well-liked boarder. The rest of the pupils stood back, sizing me up.

Although it was past time for school to open, I waited because I knew that six children from Paulina Valley, seven miles away, were also to be enrolled with me. Their school had been permanently closed during the summer when the Crook County School Board decided that it could save money by transporting the pupils to Paulina. The decision had not been a popular one with the two families involved, but it could be carried out in spite of that because

Paulina student body, 1933-34. Kneeling in front: Howard Roundtree, ? Higgins. Front row, left to right: Lawrence Higgins, ? Gardner, ? McCulloch, ? Higgins, Darrel Higgins, ? McCulloch, ? Ritzloff. At back with ball on his head, Donald Roundtree. Next, partly hidden, ? Gardner. Peeking out from behind, Louise Gardner. At end of row, Johnzie Faulkner. Three pupils were absent.

Crook County schools were in a county unit system which took away many of the local districts' prerogatives.

The carload of children finally arrived. When they came into the room, I was struck by their similarity to the pupils in my first school. The two boys from the Higgins family had unkempt hair, heavy work shoes, and faded jeans. Their two sisters, clean, faded housedresses worn with sturdy shoes also brought back memories of my first school. These children lived back on a small isolated ranch which did not provide for jaunts to Prineville, so they considered a trip to Miller's store at Paulina a trip "to town." And they probably looked upon the Paulina school as being a town school. The two McCulloch boys also came from a small ranch.

After everyone was seated, I took the roll and discovered that the sixteen youngsters were in seven different grades. Heretofore I had taught only older children, so I was troubled when I discovered that there was a six-year-old boy and two second graders in the group. There those little ones sat, trustfully expecting me to guide them through the simpler books of the Alice and Jerry reading series.

Always before there had been an extra day of vacation on the first day of school, but here the closest town was nearly sixty miles away so my pupils had already bought pencils, a tablet, and an eraser at Miller's Store just up the road, and the district's school books were on hand ready to be passed out. There was no putting it off any longer—I must start to teach them on this very first day. To put it conservatively, time passed quickly as I rushed from group to group assigning lessons, listening to recitations, and prodding those who were not yet in the mood for study.

During the noon hour I had time to catch my breath while the local children were away eating their lunches at home and the rest of us ate ours out on the front porch. The four boys from Paulina Valley gulped down their food and hurried out to spend the rest of the noon hour trying to lasso a fence post. As the sweet-faced older Higgins girls and her little sister sat near me eating in the warm sunshine, they shyly tried to visit with me. It was a restful time that ended as soon as the others came hurrying back from their nearby homes.

The rest of the day continued to be a busy time but less confusing for everyone as I began learning the pupils' names.

Soon after I dismissed school, I heard a car drive into the school grounds. When it stopped by the front steps, I went to the door and saw that one of the car's occupants was the young ranch woman who earlier had been concerned for fear I didn't have a boarding place, and now she had come to deliver some more school supplies from Mr. Baker. She brought them into the schoolhouse, at the same time telling me that her name was Almeda Laughlin and that she lived on a ranch in the Beaver Creek Valley, ten miles beyond Paulina. She was planning to teach her little daughter at home that winter, so that was the reason she had attended the class on Saturday.

As she left the schoolhouse, I followed her out to the car where she introduced me to her husband, Earl Laughlin, and their elderly passenger, Mrs. Mary Lister, who was their neighbor. Both Mr. Laughlin and Mrs. Lister climbed out of the car to shake my hand and visit with me which seemed especially courteous of Mrs. Lister who was so much older than I. Both women indicated that they wanted me to be their weekend guest later in the year. They lived ten miles away in a different school district, so it surprised me to have them showing all this friendly interest in Paulina's schoolma'am.

3

Later, as Ola and I exchanged information about past experiences I learned that her husband, Fred, had been a successful country storekeeper in various parts of Oregon and Idaho, but in each locality he grew tired of the long hours and being forced to maintain good public relations at the expense of his own good times. An example of this was going to a dance and feeling obliged to dance with a steady customer, no matter how miserably she danced.

When he grew too tired of being a storekeeper, he'd always sell out and turn to ranching. The last store he'd owned had been near Astoria in Clatsop County and now they were here in central Oregon on a small irrigated ranch trying to make a living by selling the cream from a herd of dairy cows. Farm incomes were as low in Paulina as they were every place else so that is probably the reason they took me in as a boarder at twenty dollars a month.

The Grays did not have a radio or phonograph and didn't play cards, so there was little to do after we finished reading the daily paper that came in the mail. The rest of the evening we sat and talked, which was to my liking because I was interested in learning more about this part of Oregon's cattle country.

In Paulina I had the feeling of being in open country because the little community sat at the edge of a wide valley. The cattle ranches I had seen on my way from Prineville had large, well-cared-for dwellings and barns with broad irrigated fields in the background, all of which gave an impression of past prosperity despite the ruinously low price of beef during the Depression.

Fred and Ola shared with me what they had observed personally and what had been told by March Logan, an old-timer in those parts. March had briefed Fred on every family within a thirty mile radius including not only the present generation but the one that preceded it. March, who lived in one of the nearby unpainted houses, did not have a job during the winter so he often spent the afternoons tagging after Fred and talking to him while Fred worked.

It didn't take long for me to learn the names of the ranch families and the general direction in which they lived because people were scarce in this widespread neighborhood of ranches. Six families owned irrigated places in the large and fertile Beaver Creek Valley ten miles past Paulina. There the ranch houses were within a few miles of each other, making it possible for the occupants to see smoke pouring from their neighbors' chimneys on a cold, clear winter morning. Compared to most of the cattle country, the valley was almost congested. Some of the ranches along Beaver Creek had been expanded by taking in unirrigated farms and pasture lands so they sprawled over the countryside for miles and miles with a total of fifty thousand acres.

Fred and Ola also told me about the people on those prosperous looking places that I had seen along the Crooked River on my way up from Prineville, and of other large spreads located in out-of-the-way places. Ranches varied in size and productivity, depending upon how much water they had for irrigation. The few extra large and several good sized ranches had water rights so they could raise hay for their livestock, but those living on small dry farms had only the unreliable precipitation to water their crops and pasture lands.

Talking was one way to pass the time, but what could I do in the evenings after the Grays had exhausted their store of information about the surrounding country and its inhabitants? Then I remembered reading books from the State Library in Salem while I was at Summer Lake, so I wrote to Dr. Lesch, asking him to send me a list of books by current authors.

Accommodating as always, he immediately sent me a long list of books to which I could refer throughout the winter whenever I needed to send for more reading material. An added interest was sharing the books with Ola and Fred. One of them, *An American Tragedy* by Theodore Drieser, was so long that it was hard for the three of us to find time to finish reading the book before it had to be returned. In fact, the day before I had to send it back hardworking Fred neglected his work for a whole day, hurriedly reading on and on to find out how the story ended.

That took care of what to do at home, but even before this I had

discovered that Paulina was a lively community. The first dance I
went to was an impromptu one held at the Grange hall on Friday of
the opening week of school. My trunk had gone astray so all I'd
had to wear that week were a housedress and a wool suit. In spite
of the heat I had been wearing the suit with different blouses to
school every day, so on Friday evening, in order to have a change,
I went to the dance in my gingham housedress. Ola and I walked
over without Fred who decided not to go because he was tired and
had to work the next day. Others must have felt the same way because there was a very small crowd, with the men outnumbering
the girls and women two to one. Like other members of the gentler
sex, I danced every dance and turned down more. Most of the time
I danced with Forest Service employees who worked as supervisors
at the Civilian Conservation Corps which had a camp in Ochoco
National Forest above Beaver Creek Valley.

Ola and I left early, and as I undressed for bed, it seemed to me
that the evening had been rather a humdrum one in spite of having
all my dances taken. By far, the most interesting thing that had
happened was meeting a tall, well-built young man. It was late
when he came in escorting a young lady, so I noticed them the
minute they entered the hall.

The young man didn't have the appearance of an ordinary hired
hand so I surmised that he was a rancher, but he didn't fit the
description of anyone that I'd heard about from the Grays. His
companion was wearing a long black evening dress and carried a
beaded bag. I was consumed with curiosity so between dances I
asked Ola if she knew who they were. But she too was in the dark.
For some reason, I took it for granted that they were a married
couple so I was startled when the stranger flirted with me as he
guided his dance partner close to where I was dancing.

Soon he asked me for a waltz, during which he told me that his
name was Laurence Martin and that he worked for Earl Laughlin
whose wife had brought me the books from the superintendent. In
subsequent dances I learned that he seldom went to the Paulina
gatherings, which explained why Ola had not known his name.
That evening, however, he had come to bring his friend in the long
black evening dress because she was from the Willamette Valley
and had never been to a cattle country dance. During our conversa-
tions I deduced that she had come to visit him for the weekend and
was staying at the Laughlins.

As I drifted off to sleep that night, I remembered his quiet, deep speaking voice, our dances together, and most persistent was the memory of his flirting with me even though I was wearing an unpretentious housedress.

So that was my introduction to dances at the Grange hall but the affairs there represented only one part of the social scheme. Formerly everyone in the community belonged to the Grange, but for some reason dissension developed between members who were large ranch owners and the less well-to-do—the dryland farmers, renters, and small landholders.

The big ranch families withdrew from the Grange and formed their own social club which they called the Paumau Club because its members came from the Paulina-Beaver Creek area and the Maury district. In the meantime the remaining Grange members were left in possession of the big hall so the Grange organization continued to be as active as ever.

Since Ola and Fred had moved to Paulina after the quarrel, they did not have to take sides. They were officers in the Grange and attended its social affairs. Ola met with the Paumau ladies at their monthly get-togethers and she and Fred went to Paumau social gatherings at their clubhouse, which was an unoccupied dwelling on the Harry Severence ranch. Since I lived with the Grays, I too, was considered a neutral. Although I joined the Grange, I was welcomed to all the social gatherings of the other faction.

The Paumau ladies took turns being hostess for their monthly meetings which, during the summer, were on a weekday. However, they changed to Saturday meetings after school opened so the teachers could attend. Once again I was amazed by the spirit of this example of the hospitality so evident in these ranch people in central Oregon.

Early in September Ola took me to my first Paumau Club gathering which was held at the home of Eva Severence in the Maury district. While there I met the young beginning teacher from Beaver Creek and another young girl who was teaching at an isolated ranch on the north fork of the Crooked River. Her pupils were the three children of the Teeter family whom she taught in the tiny schoolhouse out in back of the ranch house. Others at the meeting were Mrs. Miller, a gray-haired woman who was teaching the Maury school, and eight or ten ranch women, some of whom had come forty miles for this brief visit with their friends.

During the program one of the members gave a book report which the ladies could relate to because it dealt with ranch life including the busy schedule of the heroine, who was a ranch wife just as they were. The author gave a realistic account of the heroine's activities as she prepared the noon meal for a crew of hay hands and then, as she saw them coming in from the fields, bustling around to get the food on the table. I have never forgotten some of the Paumau ladies' rapt interest—especially that of our hostess. Her eyes were shining. As the speaker concluded by reading an excerpt from the story, Mrs. Severence exclaimed, "That's *exactly* the way it is here on the ranch. I could just see myself rushing around doing the very same things!"

The tale didn't appeal to me. It sounded like nothing but hard work, and although they were not mentioned in the story, I visualized the stacks of messy dishes to be washed, now that the men had devoured the food she'd slaved over. But to those women who had always lived on a ranch, it was all in a day's work and part of the life they loved.

As a Grange member I discovered that the Paumaus were not the only group that put on entertainments in conjunction with their meetings. Glee Congleton, chairman of the Grange's social committee, was disappointed when I regretfully admitted that I could not play the piano, because the organization was badly in need of a pianist. But I could carry a tune, so (according to a letter which I wrote to my family that fall) I was soon called upon to entertain my fellow Grangers.

Thursday p.m.
October 20, 1934

Dear Folks,

I have a feeling that I won't have a chance to
write to you tomorrow so, since I've just finished
making out monthly report cards, I shall use my
spare time tonight.

Tomorrow after school I'm going to walk a mile
over to Glee Congleton's ranch to practice a song.
Glee is a fortyish-year-old divorcee. She and I are
supposed to sing "Annie Laurie" and "When
You and I were young, Maggie," with Glee singing alto as I carry the tune. We have practiced a
half hour so far, so we must really work before we
perform Saturday night.

Saturday a.m.

Didn't get this letter mailed yesterday so I'll add
a bit before I carry it over to the post office at
Miller's store. It should go out on this afternoon's
stage.

I just returned from Glee's where I not only
practiced all evening but stayed overnight. The
songs are going to be a real challenge since we
have no accompaniment. Hope I don't get ner-
vous and breathless. Oh well—it's only the Grange
members and they aren't so grand. Anyway, they
are used to taking what they can get.

When it was time for our act Saturday night, Glee and I went to
the piano in one corner at the front of the hall. After she struck a
chord to give us the pitch, we walked away to stand under the hanging gasoline lantern in order to have light as we read the words
from our song books. By the time we reached the lantern, I had lost
the pitch but, full of confidence, I started to sing "Annie Laurie"
which begins on a low note and then rapidly soars to high ones.
When I came to the words, "gave me her promise true which ne'er
forgot will be," I was straining and, figuratively speaking, standing
on tiptoe in an effort to reach the high tones. In the meantime Glee
was valiantly trying to harmonize. Somehow we finished, but in do-

ing so my lyric soprano voice reached hitherto unattainable heights, which just goes to show what can be done when one is desperate. The fact that I was asked to perform again also goes to show that my opinion of the audience had been correct—they took what they could get and liked it.

Whenever Ola and I were to sing a duet, we practiced at home, trusting to luck for the right pitch, but when we performed, we took our stand under the lantern and let Glee strike the correct chord for us on the piano.

The chairman of our social committee had all sorts of innovative ideas. One time when her grown daughter, Ila, was visiting in Paulina, she and I, under Glee's direction, gave a sort of choral reading of "When the Moon Comes Over the Mountain," that year's song hit. While Ila softly played the melody—not just chording but actually reading the notes—I rhythmically said the refrain. I discovered that it was not an easy thing to do, but by that time I was a staunch believer in the philosophy that the "show must go on" so I did whatever was asked of me, even if it were something I'd never done before.

Always, after the program came to a close, it was time for those present to dance. Several Grange members could play the fiddle or an accordian, and others could play chords on the piano. So any of those who were there took turns providing the dance music. The Grange night dances were fun because everyone was there to have a good time and few, if any, were left sitting on the benches for want of a partner during a square dance. Whenever it was discovered that the last square was incomplete, upper grade youngsters and wrinkled old grandmothers were called from the sidelines to fill in.

As a square dancer I never became completely self-confident because I didn't understand the caller's jargon and consequently often didn't know what to do next. But everyone else did, so I observed them and if I were still headed in the wrong direction, someone immediately straightened me out. One tall, burly horse-wrangler frequently asked me to dance and when I became too confused, he literally lifted me up and pointed me the right way. But in spite of my ineptitude I enjoyed every minute because of the feeling of fellowship as we passed each other in the "grand right and left" and carried out the caller's other directions in time to the music. But square dances were only one kind of dancing enjoyed by the crowd. The musicians played waltzes, schottisches, polkas, the one-step, the two-step, and the John Paul Jones.

At midnight everyone stopped dancing to go with his or her partner into the adjoining dining room where a potluck supper was spread out on long tables. What an assortment of food the Grange members always provided! A few dry farm ranch wives generally brought boiled beans because beans were cheap, but others contributed meat loaves, casseroles of various kinds, cold fried chicken, and one woman's specialty was the best scalloped potatoes I'd ever tasted. All were eaten with meat sandwiches or home-baked bread and butter. After the main course there were pies and cakes, to be consumed with more cups of boiled coffee poured out of the two-gallon gray enamelware coffee pot.

As the year progressed, I saw that the public dances (those not held after a Grange meeting) followed a pattern which reminded me of Paisley. Early in the evening word was passed around among the men inside the hall that the bootlegger, or bootleggers, were outside. From then on men quietly disappeared from time to time and returned feeling light-hearted. By three or four a.m. or later—which is how long the dances lasted—a great deal of liquor had been consumed. However, all of the drinking took place outside and almost exclusively by men. As a rule they knew how much they could hold without appearing to be drunk and stopped drinking when they reached that point. One time, though, a middle-aged bachelor from the Post community made a spectacle of himself after he had gone outside once too many times. He was dancing with a short, vivacious ranch wife who had trouble being her charming self as they progressed around the floor. Her tall partner was kicking out with his long legs, knocking over chairs or catching them on the toe of his shoe to toss them into the ever-widening space around him. He was a one man show, but when he came to himself the next day and heard of his drunken antics, he was deeply ashamed. I didn't see him at any other dances the rest of the year.

The Harvest Ball in August seemed to linger in people's memories for the rest of the year. Whenever I enthusiastically remarked that I'd had an especially good time at a certain dance, I generally heard something to this effect: "If you think *that* was a good dance, you should have been at the Harvest Ball!"

So the Harvest Balls must have been something special, but the dance on Thanksgiving night was the memorable one for me. The Grange put on a play before the dance, and I had the comical role of a busybody. Fred and Ola also had parts so for a month before Thanksgiving we spent several nights a week at the hall rehearsing. For a couple of days March Logan and his son, Fisher, who were loyal Grangers, worked with Fred to build a temporary stage at the front of the hall with a dressing room on each side.

Before curtain time on the big night, Ola and I waited in one of the dressing rooms. As we sat there, we could hear one car after another stopping outside the hall. I looked out of the window and couldn't believe my eyes when I saw a steady stream of headlights coming around the curve near the schoolhouse. When I walked out on the stage for the first time, I saw people crowded together on benches that had been placed on the dance floor from wall to wall. The people who couldn't find places to sit were jammed toward the back of the hall and at the very back, next to the wall, men with children on their shoulders were standing on benches to enable the children to see over the heads of people in front.

The shock of seeing all those faces gazing at me from the darkened hall made me forget my lines momentarily but I rallied. And later, whenever I reappeared on the stage, it flattered the ham in me to hear one woman near the front exclaim, "Oh, here she comes again!"

Everyone agreed that the play was a huge success. Afterwards I heard that the audience included people from places as far away as Prineville. Our play, followed by a dance, was the only public social event taking place in all of Crook County that night. The dance was a lively one which lasted until 4 a.m. and, needless to say, everyone, including myself, had a wonderful time.

4

Since I was in Paulina to teach school, it was only natural that I spent far more time in the classroom than in merrymaking at the Grange hall. From the start, I went to school before eight o'clock so I could build a fire and have the room warm when the children arrived. The fire was needed because the altitude of Paulina is approximately 3,400 feet and frosty mornings, followed by hot afternoons, were not unusual in September.

There was no woodshed so firewood was stacked near the schoolhouse. However, some chunks left over from the previous year were scattered around in dry weeds, causing me to be terrified, at first, for fear there might be a rattlesnake lurking there, because I had seen one on a side road one day. Later I was more concerned about having to carry the heavy chunks into the schoolhouse through the rain or snow.

The sight of the dusty floor had bothered me from the very first time I entered the classroom, so one Friday evening a couple of weeks after school opened, I decided that the time had come to give it a coat of floor oil. Since this was something I had never done before, I consulted with Ola and my pupils and learned that the oil was applied with an ordinary rag mop.

As soon as the place was cleared of youngsters, I brought out a five gallon can of the thick, black fluid and poured some of it into an old washbasin I'd found in the back room. I plunged the mop into the oil until it was saturated. Taking care to keep it saturated, I went over every inch of the classroom and cloakroom floors. In my zeal I even accidentally splashed some out onto the front porch. When I had finished and was ready to leave, I looked around with satisfaction because there was such a uniformly heavy coat of oil on the floors.

On my way to school Monday morning I was grateful for the warmth of my winter coat. Nighttime temperatures had plummeted to the low teens that weekend. Upon arriving at the schoolhouse I unlocked the door and started to walk in but stopped to gaze in wonder at the cloakroom floor. A uniformly heavy coat of oil was *still* covering its surface. Then I noticed a layer of ice on the water left in the wash basin.

"*So* that's the reason why the oil hasn't soaked in," I thought. "Without a fire in the stove, the place has stayed cold all weekend."

By the time the youngsters arrived, the classroom's temperature had risen to the point where the oil was beginning to melt and be absorbed into the wood. It was still slicker than black ice so I repeatedly warned everyone to watch his step. Those who always have to learn the hard way didn't choose to heed my advice, resulting in some narrow escapes from bad spills during the day.

Toward the end of the year the schoolroom floor again looked dusty, but I didn't let it bother me. One coat of oil per year was enough for any classroom.

Soon after classes began, I knew that these youngsters were different from many of those I had taught at the logging camp. One big difference was that, with the exception of two slow learners, they were well prepared to work at their grade level. Since their previous teachers had trained them to have good study habits, I could avoid discipline problems by assigning work enough so they were too busy to get into mischief.

This was true of everyone but Darrel Higgins, a sixth grader, who seemed to be engaged in an experiment to determine just how much he could annoy me before I'd lose my temper. During the first week I tried to disarm him with all the charm I could muster, but he was unimpressed and continued to be contrary so I tried to conciliate him in other ways. Finally I had had enough so I have him a thorough shaking, which must have been what he was waiting for because he then showed me more respect.

When the children scattered to their homes after school that day, they spread the news that the school ma'am had given Darrel a shaking. Since there wasn't anything more exciting to talk about that day, people used Darrel's punishment as a topic for conversation when they talked over the party line. Thus the story spread.

Not long after that when I went to a Grange meeting, I danced with Darrel's unmarried uncle who was obviously amused and somewhat pleased that I had faced up to his strong willed nephew. I suppose that the only excuse I have for mentioning such a trivial subject as a naughty boy in the classroom is because I was surprised that the uncle's uncritical attitude seemed to be typical of the people's attitude toward corporal punishment, or for that matter, anything else that happened at school. Throughout the entire school year nobody came to the schoolhouse to complain, and there was no indication that I was being criticized behind my back. Evidently the parents had come to the conclusion that since I had been hired to teach their children, they would entrust them to my care and not interfere.

As I recall the happenings of that year, Darrel is the pupil who comes most often to mind, especially when I think of the many recesses and noon hours the pupils and I spent working in the unused classroom. After we'd taken out all the worthless junk, we had a big bonfire to dispose of whatever could be burned. The project had two beneficial results: the youngsters now had more room to play during stormy weather, and I learned that Darrel was happiest when he was working with his hands making repairs on the old schoolhouse. From then on I deliberately looked for odd jobs within his range of ability, because the easiest way to make him forget his contrariness was to put him to work with a hammer and nails.

Two or three of the boys sometimes came to school with unwashed faces as well as hands and forearms covered with grime, and hair uncombed. In order to improve their habits of good grooming and personal cleanliness, I sent away for cheap pocket combs which I gave to them. Anyone who hadn't done so at home was required to wash his hands and face as soon as he arrived at school.

One morning—just in case someone might need to wash—I put a wash basin of cold water on the stove to heat and waited for all the pupils to arrive. As the bus pupils came rushing in, I noticed that Darrel was left behind and when he entered, I immediately knew *why* they had left him behind. He reeked with the smell of skunk.

"Darrel! What in the world happened to make you smell like this?" I asked.

"Nothing, except I found a skunk in one of the traps on my trapline this morning," Darrel answered calmly, apparently surprised that I should be upset by the smell of a skunk.

I was perplexed. I couldn't send him home because he lived seven miles away in Paulina Valley, and merely washing his hands and face wouldn't solve the problem. As I stood there looking at him, I noticed his heavy work shoes and came to the illogical conclusion that they might be carrying most of the offensive scent. In fact, because of my past experience with his determined nature, I didn't rule out the possibility that he might have stomped the animal to death.

As I tried and tried to think of something on the premises that could be used to deodorize him, I remembered the bottle of formaldehyde out on the cloakroom shelf, left over from some former teacher's regime. The only way I'd ever seen the liquid used was as a preservative of specimens in a science laboratory. However, the label stated that it was also a disinfectant. In my desperation, I hoped that it might also counteract disagreeable odors. When I brought the bottle back into the classroom, I told Darrel to pour its contents full strength on his shoes. It turned out to be a waste of time, effort, and formaldehyde, but when he scrubbed his hands with warm water and a liberal amount of soap, that seemed to clear the air to some extent.

Still, I took the precaution of banishing my malodorous pupil to a table on the far side of the room and opened all the windows. Perhaps I had become accustomed to the smell of skunk, or maybe it was because pupils were complaining of the cold winter air coming into the room, but within an hour's time I closed the windows and school activities were back to normal. It was as though we had never heard of a skunk.

In spite of our differences I've always had a warm spot in my heart for Darrel. Among my souvenirs of teaching is the carefully made valentine with a quaint little cowboy on the front which he gave to me that year.

Because of the cooperative attitude of the youngsters and their parents, teaching was not such a worry to me as it had been at Wilark. But in one way it was more of a challenge because I had to teach the small first grade Gardner boy to read. I had no previous experience with beginners so I relied entirely upon the little one volume "Oregon State Course of Study for Rural Schools" to show me the way. This was during the time that the "look-say" no phonics approach to reading instruction was in vogue, and according to the course of study new words in the primer were introduced by first showing them to the learner on a big wall chart. I could understand that procedure all right, but the drawback was that I had no chart. In reply to a letter I wrote asking for a chart, Mr. Baker sent word that it was customary for teachers to furnish their own. So four dollars of my first fifty dollar pay check was spent for an Alice and Jerry reading chart.

As I tried to teach my first grader to read, I could see that learning new words by sight worked pretty well for the first month or so. But as the little stories became more difficult, it put a strain upon the child to have no other way but memorization to help him recognize the printed word. I remembered that my first grade teacher had taught me the sounds of the letters in the alphabet and after that, whenever I encountered an unfamiliar word, I used the sounds of the letters to discover for myself what the word was. So I began to teach phonics. I was no expert in either the sight method or the phonetic approach to reading, but fortunately for both of us the little boy was quick and alert so he learned in spite of having an inexperienced reading teacher.

The Crook County Unit System of Education did not spend money for such teaching aids as wall charts, but it did pay middle-aged Miss Sophia Messenger to supervise music teaching in the county schools. I met her first at the teachers' meeting in Prineville before I went out to Paulina. She then had handed me (and every other rural teacher) a packet of mimeographed songs with words and music which were to be taught in September. There was a different set of songs for each month of the year. When I had time, I looked at the songs and found that I didn't know the tunes, so I taught my pupils old favorites out of the songbook entitled *One Hundred and One Best Loved Songs.*

Early in October Miss Messenger showed up for her monthly visit before school opened one morning, which made me wonder at what hour she had left Prineville, As we chatted by the stove before the children arrived, I was enjoying her visit in spite of the disparity in our ages. After all, we were both teachers.

177

Miss Messenger's schedule called for her to visit the Suplee school (thirty miles farther on) that day, so as soon as the Paulina Valley pupils showed up, she started the music lesson even though it was not nine o'clock. She began by asking the youngsters to sing the songs on her September list and was greatly disturbed when she heard that we hadn't practiced them. When I explained that I wasn't familiar with the melodies, she informed me that I was supposed to have been teaching my pupils how to learn the tunes by reading the notes with the syllables. It was my misfortune to be teaching in a county that stressed music almost to the extent that it took precedence over every other subject. Even worse was the fact that the music supervisor went forth like an avenging angel to see that the music program was carried out. Neither rain, snow, nor hail discouraged her monthly visits over rough country roads to the remotest schools in the county.

It was several years since I'd taken piano lessons at Stanfield so I had forgotten most of what I had learned. However, I could read the notes on the staff and I knew that the syllables on the vocal scale were do-re-me, etc., and I could carry a tune. If there had been some way for me to learn the melody to the songs on the monthly lists, I probably could have faked the use of the syllables in teaching the songs and thus sent our visitor away smiling. As it was, she always left our school feeling displeased with me because I had done such a poor job of carrying out her lesson plan. As a rule she made no effort to conceal her feelings, but I didn't feel too squelched because I did my best (even though I wasn't adequate in music) and I knew my pupils were receiving a good education in all the other subjects.

The entire experience was a revealing one. In August I had wept bitter tears upon learning that I once again was destined to teach a one-room school. I felt that I, having earned a bachelor's degree, was too good for such a lowly position. But it took only one or two encounters with the music supervisor to show me that I wasn't as over-qualified as I had supposed I was.

5

In the meantime I was discovering that some young (*very young*) unattached men were to be found in the neighborhood. Early in October the March Logan family returned from Lake County where March and his son, Fisher, had worked at putting up hay on the ZX Ranch while Mrs. Logan cooked for the hay hands. In a letter to my family I told them about Fisher Logan.

> October 10, 1933
>
> I've found a playmate now in the person of a nice twenty-year-old boy who has just come back from haying in Paisley where he knew all the Fosters. It was *more fun* to hear of Leona, Dora, and Annie, my first pupils, being married and their brother, Ross, being a mature cow wrangler.
>
> We went to his uncle's ranch for dinner last Sunday and afterwards rode horseback through pine forests. Fisher said he stayed way behind me when we galloped so he could laught at me undisturbed. My, how I did bounce! (But I'm sure it must have been the horse's fault.) I enjoyed the ride anyway becaue it was late in the afternoon and the sunset was *beautiful.*

When Fisher's name again appeared in that letter, I was telling my parents about the radio I'd bought with the last of my college fund.

> Last night Fisher assembled the radio which came in the mail yesterday. While I was reveling in the joy of hearing orchestra music once again, the thing went *dead.* Both Fred and Fisher have looked it over carefully since then but can't find any loose connections so it must be something more serious. I guess I'll have to send it back to Montgomery Ward's to have it fixed.
>
> What a disappointment when we were all so pleased! Fred's and Ola's eyes were shining as

> much as mine probably were. When the first sta-
> tion came in, Fisher looked as if he had just seen
> Santa Claus, but oh me! it was all too brief.
> I hope Montgomery Ward's don't substitute it
> for another one because this one has a much better
> tone than some of their radios.

Fisher continued to live in Paulina most of that school year but he quit favoring me with his attention after I started to go out with men who were more mature. There were several in this category who attended the dances, mostly unmarried owners of small ranches. Occasionally one of them had the courage to ask me to go to a dance with him, but for a while my most frequent escort was a supervisor at the Civilian Conservation Corps camp beyond Paulina. He had a wealth of amusing stories to tell about the boys at the C.C.C. camp who, being from the lower east side in New York City, found living in a forest camp so far from home a bewildering experience. Even the work they did—constructing cattle guards in lieu of gates along the roads in the forest and hollowing out logs to make drinking troughs for cattle—was foreign to anything they had ever known. They couldn't comprehend the great distances between towns in this region, so whenever they had a day off, they headed for the bright lights of Prineville. Since it was approximately eighty miles away and they were on foot, sunset found them scattered for miles along the road out in the middle of nowhere. Each time this happened camp officials had to go forth with a truck to gather them up.

In that day of greater formality, the supervisor and I never did get on a first name basis even though we attended several dances together during October. He was transferred when the C.C.C. camp closed down the last of October, but by that time Laurence Martin, whom I had first met in September, showed up at a dance.

When he came over to where I was sitting, he told me that he had been on a month's vacation visiting his father and three married sisters who lived near Corvallis in the Willamette Valley. During one of our dances together, I began to think that we might have a lot in common after I heard him say that all three of his sisters were teachers and that his mother also had taught during the last years of her lifetime. With four teachers in his immediate family, Laurence, unlike many young men in those days, was neither in awe of teachers nor prejudiced against them. As far as he was concerned, they were just like anyone else, which is probably the reason I felt so at ease with him.

During the evening I mentioned that a radio had been repaired and returned to me by Montgomery Ward's and how much I enjoyed having it back. Laurence was interested, probably because so few people in the community had one. Then I did something completely out of character for me: I took the initiative by asking him if he would like to come listen to the radio. He accepted my invitation and on the following Sunday he came to see me. (And as I write, "came to see me," I do so judiciously because we both knew we were using the radio as an excuse for his visit.)

When he arrived, I took him into Grays' dining room where I kept the radio, but reception was worse than usual so we sat and talked with Ola and Fred until they retired. My visitor stayed on for a while, and as he was leaving I agreed to go to the next dance with him.

After he was gone, I tried to analyze my feelings. I found this virile young man more interesting than anyone else in Paulina who had asked me for a date (which didn't have much significance) and his age being nearly the same as mine was fitting. I liked his good manners and the fact that he was tall and slim and he wore his clothes well. Then, too, I had noticed the Model A Ford coupe that he drove which was a big improvement over a Model T roadster. I was looking forward to our date—and would have been absolutely crushed if he hadn't asked me for one—but still, I felt calm and collected. After all, we were just going to a dance, and there was nothing especially remarkable about that or the person who was taking me.

We went as planned and afterwards, back at my boarding place, we stepped into the front hall out of the cold to exchange a few last words. Although I had had a good time, I thought of my escort as merely being an agreeable, easy-to-talk-to young man.

He kissed me. Suddenly I knew how mistaken I had been. Here was someone quite extraordinary. This young man could make me feel as I had never felt before!

We began to see each other regularly. Not only did we go to all the dances, but Laurence (whom I never did call "Mr. Martin") was coming to the house on Wednesday evenings and Sunday afternoons. I seldom built a fire in the parlor stove because I had such a close friendship with Fred and Ola that I thought it would seem rude of me to leave them and take my company off to another room. We all chatted until the Grays went to bed at 8:45, so by 10 p.m. when Laurence rose to leave we really hadn't had much time to ourselves during the evening.

181

Laurence Martin

There were no scenic drives around Paulina and during that time of year the roads were often nothing but muddy trails. But whenever the weather permitted, Laurence and I went for a ride in order to be alone to talk and gain a better understanding of each other.

Laurence told me that he was in central Oregon because he could earn more working as a ranch hand than he could at any job to be found around Corvallis. He had come to this particular part of

182

the cattle country because his mother was a member of one of the well-known ranch families of central Oregon. Her father, Thomas Lister, had homesteaded a ranch on the north fork of the Crooked River in the 1860s and later, when her brother Hugh Lister struck out for himself, he settled on Beaver Creek. Throughout the years Hugh Lister increased his holdings until he had one of the biggest ranches in that part of the state. After his death in the late 1920s, his son Robert took over the management.

Laurence Martin and Grace Brandt on Listers' front porch

I asked Laurence why he hadn't gone to work for his uncle when he came to Paulina looking for a job. It seemed to me that would have been the natural thing to do, but Laurence said he took a job with Earl Laughlin, whose place adjoined the Listers', because he didn't want to feel obliged to relatives.

In most ways our backgrounds were quite different. I had been brought up in the suburbs of Portland but he had always lived on a farm. I didn't have to be unusually perceptive to see that his primary interests were related to the out-of-doors. He liked to hunt and fish and he had an extensive knowledge of anything pertaining to wildlife.

183

Ever since the first grade I had either been going to school or teaching children so most of my life had been oriented towards education. Laurence had not wanted to go to college, in spite of the urging of his parents who thought he should enroll in engineering because of his aptitude for mathematics. To Laurence it had seemed more important to go to work so he could have spending money right away. I couldn't understand this point of view and it bothered me.

Even though I was strongly attracted to Laurence, I was striving to keep my wits about me and not be swept away by emotion. In order to learn his reading tastes I loaned him some of the library books I was reading. When he was through with a book, I didn't go so far as to actually quiz Laurence about it but I gathered from his remarks that he enjoyed the novels and that they weren't over his head. Then when he mentioned the books he and Mr. and Mrs. Laughlin had read to learn about the geological history of the Paulina country, I knew that he was not an illiterate. (I wonder to whom but a school teacher this would have mattered so much.)

One time Laurence's aunt, Mrs. Mary Lister, who had been so cordial when she stopped by the schoolhouse the first day of school, told me how found she had been of Laurence's mother, whose fundamental goodness had earned the liking and respect of everyone who knew her. This helped me to understand the background for Laurence's quiet air of refinement and decency of which I had been aware from the start. It also explained why he took it for granted that I would have high standards without my having to make an issue of it.

Preparations for Christmas were undemanding that year. There was no reason for a school program because the community's need for entertainment was taken care of so effectively by the Grange. However the Paumau ladies were planning a Christmas bazaar and party at their clubhouse so I knew I would be expected to take something to be sold. Even though my fudge didn't always harden, sometimes necessitating the use of a spoon, I decided that I would take candy to the Paumau Christmas sale. This time, however, I would try to make a different kind, a delicious toffee-like candy that was Ola's specialty. I expected her to help me make it, but she and Fred made one of their rare trips to Prineville that Saturday so

I was on my own. This time I was determined to have a candy that was thoroughly cooked, so I let it boil and boil with the result that when I poured it out, it was overdone and threatening to turn to sugar. It wasn't a total failure, but the texture was far from perfect.

When Laurence stopped by to take me to the party that evening, he sampled a piece of the candy while I looked on, painfully conscious of its imperfections. Later I placed it on the sales table at the Paumau clubhouse as unobtrusively as possible in hopes that no one would notice who had put it there. That others had been there before me was apparent from the assortment of goodies on display—nutty chocolate and divinity fudges, caramels, penuche, and peanut brittle, all obviously made by experts.

During the time set aside for the sale of bazaar items, I stayed away from the candy table, but when I heard my escort being teased, I looked over in that direction. I shall never forget my sense of gratitude when I saw that Laurence had gallantly purchased every bit of my candy.

In contrast to the Grange, many of the Paumau Club members—even some of the men—could play the piano, which meant that the latest dance songs were played at their parties. That night Laurence and I danced to the currently popular song, "Did You Ever See a Dream Walking?" Its chorus had this romantic ending:

> "And the dream that was walking
> And the dream that was talking
> And the heaven in my arms was you."

I was familiar with the song from having heard it on the radio and had liked it, but after the Paumau party, it had a special meaning for me. I associated it with Laurence and dancing in his arms.

When it was time for me to go home for Christmas, I found a ride with a young ranch hand who was going to spend the holidays with his parents in the Willamette Valley. He thought he could make some extra money by taking me along as a passenger. I was in favor of the idea because it was much less expensive and complicated than riding the afternoon stage from Paulina to Prineville and then waiting in Prineville until I could catch a bus for Portland.

As usual, it was good to be home among my friends and family once more. I looked up Leib and Sylvia Riggs, who were living in Portland by then, and learned that Sylvia was planning a New Year's Eve party. I hurriedly wrote to Ola, asking her to send my evening dress and matching slippers so I could wear them to the party, which she did. She told Laurence about my request when she saw him at the Grange dance on New Year's Eve, so the first time he came to see me after school reopened, he teased me about having to send all the way to Paulina for something to wear.

I said little to my family, and even less to Sylvia, about the young man in the cattle country whom I was seeing so regularly. As a matter of fact, there wasn't much to tell because I had known him such a comparatively short time. Nevertheless, I bought the sheet music to "Did You Ever See a Dream Walking?" so Clarice could play it on the piano. When we sang it together as we did so often while I was home, my thoughts were always far, far away in Paulina.

6

When it became common knowledge that Laurence and I were going together, I began to get invitations from Mrs. Robert Lister, better known as "Hazel," to spend the weekend with them. I suppose there was some sense of family loyalty involved since Laurence was her husband's cousin.

I always looked forward to those visits not only because of the relaxed air of western hospitality but because I enjoyed the big ranch house which had all the conveniences to be found in a fine urban home. Then too, the Listers hired a woman to do the cooking and kitchen work so Hazel was free to entertain and help me with the sewing I was doing for myself after Christmas. Having attended a private boarding school and being a graduate of Oregon Agricultural College, she had acquired some sewing skills along the way so she helped me make two or three good-looking dresses that spring.

The household included Robert and Hazel Lister, their two little daughters, and the grandmother, Mrs. Mary Lister, who had been mistress of this house while her husband was alive. The Beaver Creek school teacher, Ina Roberts, boarded with them, so she too, was there when I was a guest at the ranch.

I felt much, much older than this young teacher fresh out of normal school who was in love with Dick Hicks, one of Listers' ranch hands. Dick was an experienced cow wrangler in his late twenties who had no means of transportation but his riding horse, so occasionally Laurence took them along when we went to a dance. It was crowded in the Model A coupe, but Ina didn't mind that at all. As I observed her obvious infatuation for this good-looking, somewhat older cowboy who could dance so divinely, I was pretty sure that, as far as Dick's literary tastes were concerned, she couldn't care less. She was head over heels in love with him and that was all that counted.

Whenever I met Almeda Laughlin, who was Laurence's employer's wife, we always had much to talk about. Not only had she been a public school teacher but even then was teaching her little daughter at home in order to avoid the daily bother of transporting her to and from the Beaver Creek School.

During the Paumaus' Christmas party Almeda had tentatively set the date for me to be their weekend guest, and from then on for several weeks after the holidays she made arrangements for me to come on a certain date, only to have to call my visit off. First, her children were sick, and then for a month the roads were so bad that she was afraid to drive to Paulina to pick me up. But early in February we had a spell of springlike weather so I finally went to see them.

Earl and Alameda, who had met in Prineville where she taught school and he owned a garage, were married just before Earl came back to this community to take over his father's ranch on Sugar

Creek. He made improvements on the ranch, including renovating and enlarging the ranch house, the core of which was the original log cabin built in pioneer times.

Almeda, who loved to garden, was a native of western Washington where rainfall is plentiful and flowers, green vegetation, and beautiful gardens abound. The only plants that she could use in Paulina were those that could survive the high altitude and wintertime lows that sometimes reached 57° below zero, but she managed to find them and after several years she had the beauty spot she had envisioned. While I was there, Almeda laughingly told me how Laurence had shared in the yard beautification project. Whenever he went fishing he dug for worms along the inside of the fence which enclosed the plot of ground around the house. In this painless manner the borders for flowers and ornamental shrubs were gradually enlarged.

The Saturday afternoon of my visit word came from a ranch down the road a few miles that Laughlins' mail was there waiting to be picked up. After dinner Laurence used that as an excuse for us to get away and go for a short moonlight ride. (It had to be short because Earl was an inveterate tease, and if we stayed away too long, he would make us the butt of his jokes for the rest of the evening.) Upon our return I joined the others in the living room, but Laurence went into the kitchen to read the letter addressed to him.

On our way back to Grays' the next afternoon, Laurence told me the contents of the letter—at least the part that would interest me. His father would have to repossess a farm because the people to whom he had sold it in the early 1920s were unable to pay off the mortgage, and now he wanted Laurence to come back to western Oregon to help him run it. The news disturbed me, but Laurence hadn't made up his mind yet so I hoped for the best.

A couple of weeks later when Laurence arrived for his usual Sunday afternoon visit, I could see that he had been doing some serious thinking. He had finally come to the conclusion that it was his duty to help his father, which meant that he would leave Paulina. And he had also been giving some serious thought to our relationship so that same afternoon he asked me to marry him. I can't say that I was surprised. I had already come to the realization of how empty my life would be if I were never to see him again, so he didn't have to wait long for his answer.

Being one of those people who made their marriage plans during the Depression, I was deprived of the light-hearted confidence in the future felt by prospective brides in normal times. The 280-acre farm that his father was repossessing in one of the coastal valleys, plus a herd of dairy cows would ordinarily provide a fairly good income, but these were not normal times. Most school boards were not hiring married women so that ruled out the possibility of my contributing to our income, so the future looked bleak.

Still, when I asked Laurence if the thought of supporting a wife frightened him, he said, "No." I ought to have known that if it had, he wouldn't have proposed to me.

I wrote to tell my family and a few friends that I was engaged to be married, but no one in the Paulina area except Ola and Fred knew of our commitment. The people there were so curious about each other's business that it had become second nature for us to be secretive. The only reason I told Ola was because I was certain that she would not betray my confidence, and besides, I was bursting to talk to someone about the matter. When Robert and Hazel Lister had a farewell party for Laurence just before he left in the middle of March, everyone there watched us closely, trying to determine the status of our relationship. We let them keep on wondering.

The night before Laurence went away we still didn't know when we could be married because there was no place on his father's farm for us to set up housekeeping. The farmhouse had four bedrooms, making it large enough for us to live there with Laurence's father and stepmother, but the idea didn't appeal to either of us—especially to me. We had to wait and hope that Laurence could scrape up enough money to build us a place of our own, and if it turned out that we didn't have enough money to marry, I would teach another year.

I went to the Grange meetings occasionally after Laurence left but seldom attended the dances because the Grange members didn't consider me a neutral observer in the Paumau-Grange feud after I started going out with Laurence. Not only was he related to the Listers, but he worked for the Laughlins who were also Paumaus.

So the Grangers who had always danced with me before no longer came around asking for dances. That hadn't fazed me when I was there with Laurence, but after he went away I missed the Grange members' friendship.

March 24, 1934

> Dear Laurence,
> While the rest of the good Paulinaites are making merry at Post, their school ma'am, who is in disgrace it seems, stays home and listens to the radio. Fred thought he was being awfully funny when he told Fisher that I was anxiously waiting for a way to go to the dance. Fisher merely grinned and said, "It looks like some of these young fellows around here would ask her."
> I could skin Fred alive for giving Fisher that chance to gloat over me. Anyway, I really don't care much about the Post dances—sour grapes.

A few weeks later I again touched on the subject as I wrote to Laurence:

> Ina and Dick caught a ride to the dance with the man who is taking your place at Laughlins, so they came over from the hall to get me to go back to the dance with them. (They said they knew how it was, me without a man, etc.) When I walked into the Grange Hall with them, I didn't know if my stock with the Grangers would go up or even farther down, knowing as I did what they think of Dick Hicks.
> The dance wasn't bad but I didn't get much of a thrill out of the evening because my good old standby partners weren't there. The Grangers gave me the "go-by" until very late in the evening when Fisher Logan came over for a dance. Dick almost spoiled it all by dancing close to us all the time so he could nudge me to show me how very happy he was that the Grangers were taking me back into the fold again. At midnight Dick took both Ina and me to supper—having *much* to say about the matter.

7

During the month of March I was notified that I had been rehired to teach the Paulina school. Since our marriage plans were so indefinite, I signed the contract and felt no qualms about being unfair to the district. I knew that any number of teachers could be found to take my place, no matter how late in the summer I might resign.

One Saturday in April the women in the Paumau Club gave a bridge-tea in honor of the four teachers in the area. Since Ina was going to be teaching nearer Prineville in the six-room school at Powell Butte the following year, it was also a farewell party for her. She had told me that she was reluctant to go because of leaving Dick, but Miss Messenger had recommended her for the better position (Ina was an excellent music teacher) so she could not turn it down.

We had no way of knowing that most of those attending the party would never see Ina again. That summer she suffered a heart attack and suddenly died. Before this happened, she and Dick had slipped away to be married in Vancouver, Washington, and later I heard from Ola who had talked with them on the streets in Prineville. She wrote that Ina was bubbling over with happiness just like a little child that day, which made it even more of a shock to hear of her death a couple of months later. But remembering her earlier happiness, I thought, "At least she was Dick's wife for a little while, and for anyone as much in love as she was, that would be the fulfillment of her heart's desire."

No great celebration marked the end of the school year—not even a picnic—because the Grange took care of the community's social life. I was glad that it did. After the schoolhouse was put in order for the summer—desks emptied, textbooks stacked neatly according to subject matter, floor swept, and waste paper burned, I dismissed the children for the day and, incidentally, the year. Carrying a few of my own school belongings which had been discovered among school materials as we cleared the room, I locked the schoolhouse door one last time. I walked away, uncertain as to whether or not I would be back in the fall.

SUMMER, 1934

Meanwhile, long before the end of April, I had received the good news from my fiance that he was working for his brother-in-law who was part owner of a small logging operation in Harlan where Laurence now lived. In his letters Laurence told of helping his father milk the herd of dairy cows night and morning and putting in the spring crops during the weekends, so I knew he was busy.

Nevertheless, he was planning to come to Paulina after school was out so he could take me home and meet my family. That was the way we planned the weekend, but our plans went awry when Laurence had car trouble just as he reached the Severence ranch below Paulina Friday evening. He stayed there that night after sending to Prineville for a car part which would arrive late Saturday. Repairs on the car were not completed until Sunday afternoon, making it Monday before we could leave. This delay was further complicated by the fact that the telephone system in the Paulina area was a local one, not connected with the outside world, making it impossible for either of us to let our families know why we weren't arriving on schedule. Since jobs were hard to find and he would have already been absent one day without notice, Laurence thought we should go directly to Harlan where he could be on hand to work Tuesday. Therefore, I ended up going to his home instead of Laurence coming to mine.

It was raining a steady downpour late that afternoon as we left U.S. Highway 30 at Burnt Woods and turned onto a graveled road which led to Harlan six miles back in the Coast Range Mountains. The road wound through rugged, sometimes timbered country, descending rapidly for a spell, then following along a creek through small level pockets in the hills, where sheep and goats were grazing. Occasionally we passed a farm house perched on a hillside or nestled in a small glen. In some places the road was built out of the hillside along the creek, on the other side of which were steep mountains. At last we rounded a curve and entered a large, open valley. The nearby store building had a sign indicating that the Harlan post office was inside so I knew we were at the center of the community. In less than five minutes we reached Martins' farm house.

When Laurence pulled up to the gate, I saw fruit trees and ornamental shrubs growing in the midst of the waist high grass which almost hid the fence around the yard. Water dripped from every leaf and every blade of grass. Coming directly from Paulina as I had, it was hard for me to adjust to the typical western Oregon springtime display of rampantly growing vegetation. It struck me as being undisciplined and overdone. Furthermore, all the wetness depressed me.

Soon after we entered the house, I realized that coming in unexpectedly about supper time was no way to be assured of an enthusiastic welcome. Laurence's stepmother, who was in her late fifties, had done the week's washing the hard way that day, scrubbing the clothes on a washboard. She was tired and had intended to have a light evening snack of leftovers from the hearty midday meal. Now that was impossible. Soon after we arrived, she went to the kitchen to prepare a complete meal and later, with obvious weariness she went upstairs to make up the bed in one of the spare bedrooms for me. I felt guilty because I knew I was the cause of all this extra work. It was not an auspicious first meeting with my future in-laws.

While Laurence was at work the next day, I spent the time becoming acquainted with his father and stepmother and looking out at the rain-drenched landscape. The farm was centrally located with the store and post office only a short walk down the road and directly across from the farm house I could see a small unpainted store building now used as a dwelling. Adjoining its yard were the schoolgrounds for Harlan's two-room school, and farther up the road another farm house.

That evening Laurence took me out to Corvallis where I spent the night at the home of his oldest sister, Dorothy Allison. The next morning I boarded the bus for Portland and a few hours later was once again back with my family.

At home again, I took stock of my financial situation and was convinced that teaching in an isolated community had its advantages. Except for the monthly charge of twenty dollars for room and board, there had been few expenses, and nothing but mail order catalogs to tempt me to spend the rest of my monthly earnings. Therefore, out of the four hundred dollars received for teaching eight months, I had saved almost two hundred, and the Crook County school district, which paid on a twelve months basis, still owed another two hundred dollars. If I were to resign to be married (or for any other reason) I would receive that amount in a lump sum.

As I studied the advertisements in the Portland papers, I saw that furniture was being sold at rock-bottom prices so I rushed downtown to take advantage of a sale which offered walnut veneer four-piece bedroom suites for seventy-five dollars. When they turned out to be of an excellent quality, I bought one and was extremely proud of my purchase. Later I heard from a friend who worked in the Doernbecher furniture factory where the bedroom set was made, that it was the company's top brand and then I was even more pleased. A box spring and innerspring mattress set cost twenty dollars, and the pillows, bed linen, blankets, and bedspread that I bought were commensurately priced.

Our prospects for finding a place to live looked brighter when Laurence learned that the little store building across the road from Martins' house would soon be vacated and put up for rent. I responded to Laurence's suggestion that we might use it temporarily by writing back.

> I think the store is the solution to our problem. Never will furniture be so cheap again so my savings can go a long way. By combining what you and I have, we can get along fine. As you must know by now from having read my letter full of the subject, I bought a *goodlooking* bedroom set. If we could find some more bargains like that in other pieces of really nice furniture, we could make any little shack into a place we can be proud of. With fresh paper on the walls, paint, cute curtains, plus the elegant furniture, just think what a love nest our home will be!

Because we knew in our hearts that it would be foolish to put our marriage off another year, we decided to be married in June. I sent in my letter of resignation and received a check for two hundred dollars. Now I *really* was on the prowl for bargains that would make our home into "a thing of beauty and a joy forever." Meier & Frank advertised a sale of davenport and chair sets for forty-eight dollars with values up to one hundred and forty dollars. But the ad was honest enough to state that just *one* set had formerly been priced that high. On the morning of the sale I was at the store early, waiting in front of the crowd of other shoppers for the doors to open. Once inside, I dashed from place to place looking at price tags until I found the drastically reduced (but perfectly good) davenport and chair which were destined to add to the comfort of our home for many a year.

Another time I found a sale on imported English dishes of excellent quality. A complete service for six, including extra pieces not found in present-day sets, cost sixteen dollars. Laurence gave me money to buy Community silverplated flatware which my sister-in-law's brother secured for me at wholesale prices. In addition, he and his wife gave us a set of matching salad forks. And so, every week found more added to our store of household goods.

In the midst of all these preparations for setting up housekeeping, my fiance and I were able to see each other only two times. He endured the experience of being inspected by all the members of my family—and passed the test with flying colors. Then early in June I went to Harlan for a second visit.

This time the weather was heavenly. There had been a respite from spring rains so grass along the fence rows had been brought under control and the Martins' front yard was neatly mowed. The weather was so pleasant during the weekend that doors and windows could be left open letting in the fragrance of honeysuckle. Laurence's stepmother, who was prepared for this visit, was at her charming best, and she and Laurence's father did their best to make me feel at home.

Sunday morning Laurence asked me to go with him while he attended to his father's band of sheep pastured in the hills across the river. To get there, we walked along the banks of the Big Elk River, which bordered the farm's bottom lands on two sides, and crossed

over to the brushy hillside by means of an old log bridge. As I tried
to keep up with Laurence climbing so effortlessly along the trails, I
begged him to stop every once in a while so I could rest. Then I
would look back to the peaceful beauty of the valley with its green
pastures and grain fields in view. The unfavorable impression of
Harlan carried away from that unscheduled visit in April could not
hold out against the magical spell of this perfect June day.

Prior to my visit Laurence had written to tell me of his intentions
to build us a small house instead of renting the store building. He
could buy the lumber at the local mill and his three brothers-in-law
would come to Harlan some weekend to help him built it.
However, the house-raising could not take place until August, after
the hay crop was harvested, and there were fewer demands from
the farm for Laurence's time. So we'd have to live with Laurence's
father and stepmother for awhile.

Before Laurence took me out to Corvallis Sunday evening, we
chose a building site among the fruit trees a short distance from the
farm house. As we talked about a "small house" which seemed to
be on our minds so much of the time, I envisioned Mary Troy's
camp house at Wilark, and I told Laurence I'd like a house with a
similar floor plan. He agreed that it would be easy to build and promised me that if that was what I wanted, that's what we'd have. As
we drove away from the farm house that Sunday evening I felt as
lighthearted and carefree as a prospective bride is supposed to feel.

Laurence didn't want a large wedding, and I was not one who
had dreamed all her life of walking down the church aisle in a veil
and gown, so I didn't really care one way or the other. I could even
accept the idea of our being married by a justice of the peace, but
my mother couldn't. She wanted us to have a home wedding with a
religious ceremony because she wanted me to have the memory of
becoming Laurence's wife in a loving atmosphere among people
who cared about us. I argued that it would cost too much to serve
refreshments to a houseful of people, and besides that, Laurence
and I wouldn't know where to stop if we once started making out a
guest list. We'd either end up with a large crowd or hurt some feel-

ings by leaving people out. A compromise was reached by inviting only the members of our immediate families, including, of course, the spouses and children. I sent out formal announcements to people who would be interested to learn of our marriage.

Next, my mother began to fret because I was planning on being married in an ordinary street length summer dress because I thought anything dressy that I might buy for the wedding probably would never be used again. Finally, I agreed to borrow Clarice's organdy party dress which I wore with the corsage of dainty roses Laurence brought me, thus ending up dressed as Mama had wanted me to be.

The ceremony took place under a big dogwood tree in the natural wooded setting of my brother's back yard. As the wedding was on Saturday, a work day, only four members of Laurence's family came to join mine for the wedding so there was only a small crowd of eighteen people to share the buffet luncheon my sister-in-law served.

According to pictures taken that day, I was almost too radiant, while Laurence, on the other hand, was terribly serious, almost dejected-looking, which puts me on the defensive whenever I see people gazing at our wedding pictures. I hasten to assure them that Laurence was there of his own free will, that I had not—as the picture suggests—dragged him before the preacher after tracking him down.

After living with Laurence's folks a couple of months, we moved into the unpretentious little house which followed the same floor plan as Mary Troy's. As I looked around, I fully realized that it had none of the studied charm of her place, but nevertheless I was content with what I saw. There, outside the window, were the pink geraniums in a window box, a wedding present to us from friends who owned a nursery. The pretty sets of dishes and stemware, also wedding presents, were displayed in the open kitchen cupboards my father had built for us when he and my mother came for a visit. For weeks wedding gifts trickled in from our friends and relatives in various parts of the state. Some of them were concrete manifestations of the friendliness I had encountered so often during my years as a teacher.

It was pleasing to be reminded of those friendships and experiences in different parts of Oregon, but now I had something far better. I had found that which I'd been seeking a long time: a husband I could trust, one who accepted and appreciated me just the way I was—old-fashioned moral values and all. I felt that Laurence was innately honest and sincere and I had no fears for the permanence of our marriage.

At last we were in our own home and as I counted my blessings, that which came to mind first of all was the knowledge that we were deeply in love.

Laurence and Grace on their wedding day, June 30, 1934

REFLECTIONS

I have finally come to the end of the second volume of events in my life as a teacher from 1926 to 1934, and now I must take stock of my writing effort. During the early part of the narrative, I found myself smiling at how surprised my three grandchildren—who were little children when I started these memoirs—would be to learn that their grandma had ever had some of the experiences I was relating. So I suppose that at first I was merely trying to tell an interesting story.

Then the old instinct to teach took over. I began to think how important it is for the younger generation to know history—even that as comparatively recent as fifty years ago. By knowing what people were doing and thinking in the past, they can come to a better understanding of the present. As I told of the hardships and anxieties as well as the good times, I hoped that it would be apparent that this day and age does not have a monopoly on reasons to feel tense and apprehensive.

Further on in my reminiscences, I realized that some things never change. Way back then I was made to feel silly because I was holding out for my ideals. The arguments used in an effort to persuade me that I was wrong sounded logical and reasonable and I suspect that about the same line of reasoning could be used today when an attempt is made to undermine an idealist's convictions.

It was just as well that I was not overly anxious to be married, so I did not grab the first opportunity for matrimony. Now I can see how many interesting times I might have missed, and how much more narrow my outlook would probably have been if I had married and settled down after teaching one year at Summer Lake. Sometimes I flinched when an older matron "tsk tsked" and marveled that I was still unmarried at the age of twenty-five, but nowadays I treasure those years which gave me an opportunity to develop and find myself before I became part of another individual's life.

What seemed remarkable is that each time I started to write about a different community, I became so engrossed that I felt as if I were back in that place and time. My heart ached for the disillusioned, still very young, girl in that drafty little shack at Summer Lake, and I was bitter as I thought of the people who had caused her disillusionment.

Writing about my sojourn in the logging camp five years later, I enjoyed the independence of the poised young woman I had come to be. And I gave her credit for systematically putting aside money to be used for a year at the university despite her weakness for fashionable clothes. So it was, each time I told about my experience in a new setting.

As I wrote, I found that I was in two roles. Even while one part of me was totally involved in reliving my experiences, another part was taking an objective view of those past events and the people associated with them. Consequently, I have gained a better understanding of myself and others, especially my parents. Whenever I think of my mother, I now have a greater appreciation for her wisdom, courage in adversity, and devotion to her children.

I was continually enrolling in college classes during the latter part of my teaching career—a whole year of regular session, working for a Master's degree, followed by numerous summer sessions and night classes, all with the purpose of gathering more knowledge so I could become a better teacher. Now in writing these memoirs I have discovered another means of learning—this time for my own enrichment.

Of all that I've learned, probably what has been most rewarding is to have come to the realization of how much good I experienced during those early years. Wherever I went I always found friends. As I remember this blessing, any bad memories I might have been harboring no longer seem important. Compared to the good memories I have recently unearthed, the bad ones are nothing but nebulous shadows.